G000256262

HAUNTED SCOTLAND

Also by Norman Adams

Non-fiction
Goodbye, Beloved Brethren
Dead and Buried?
In the Dead of the Night!
Hangman's Brae
Haunted Valley
Haunted Neuk
Scotland's Chronicles of Blood

Fiction
Bloody Tam (with Ninian Reid)
Blood Dirk

Haunted Scotland

NORMAN ADAMS

MAINSTREAM
PUBLISHING

EDINBURGH AND LONDON

Copyright © Norman Adams, 1998
All rights reserved
The moral right of the author has been asserted

First published in Great Britain in 1998 by
MAINSTREAM PUBLISHING COMPANY (EDINBURGH) LTD
7 Albany Street
Edinburgh EH1 3UG

ISBN 1 85158 952 X

No part of this book may be reproduced or transmitted in any form or by any
means without written permission from the publisher, except by a reviewer who
wishes to quote brief passages in connection with a review written for insertion
in a magazine, newspaper or broadcast

A catalogue record for this book is available from the British Library

Typeset in Garamond
Printed and bound in Great Britain by J.W. Arrowsmith Ltd

CONTENTS

ACKNOWLEDGEMENTS

I visited many haunted places and interviewed scores of people in connection with this book. I acknowledge with deep gratitude all those persons, including those who willingly talked to me but wished to remain anonymous, who gave their time and assistance unstintingly.

Special mention must go to my fellow members of the Scottish Society for Psychical Research, Mrs Daphne Plowman and her husband John, Mrs Tricia Robertson and Professor Archie E. Roy; June, Marchioness of Aberdeen and Temair; Mr Neil M. Anderson; The Laird of Balgonie and Eddersgoll; Mrs Valerie Blaxter; Miss Judith Bowers, Spirit of Glasgow Tour Company; Brodie of Brodie; Mrs Livonia Cameron and family; Mr David Colman; Mrs Anne Craig; Dr Edwin A. Dawes and Mr Mac Wilson, of The Magic Circle; Mr David Duff; Fiona Duff, Festival Theatre, Edinburgh; Colonel Angus Fairrie; Judith and Andrew Fisken, Friends of Rosslyn; Mr Mark Fraser; Mr George Gordon; Mr Ron Halliday, Scottish Earth Mysteries Research; Patricia and John Hayton; Miss Elizabeth Honeyman; Mr David Hunt; Judith and Peter Jones; Mr Robert Kennedy; Mr Stephen Knowles; Mrs Christina McDonald; Mr Donnie McInnes, *Stornoway Gazette*; General Sir Jeremy Mackenzie; Major Malcolm Macrae, Mrs Gretta Manson; Mr Ralph Mellon, *East Fife Mail*, Montrose Aerodrome Museum Society; Mr David Morgan, *Forres Gazette*; Mrs Diane Morgan; Mr A. Gordon Morison; Mrs Mary Ellen Odie; Mr Peter Pryce, Theatre Royal, Glasgow; Mr Ninian Reid; Mrs Clare Russell; Shetland Archives (Mr Brian Smith and Mr

Angus Johnson); Clare Simpson, Royal Lyceum, Edinburgh; Mrs Geraldine Simpson; Anna Steven, *Fife Free Press*; Mr Alasdair Steven; Mrs Susannah Stone; Mr Ian Strachan; Baroness Strange; Faye Thomson, *Alloa and Hillfoots Advertiser*; Mr Frank Thompson; Miss Morag Thompson; Mr James Usher Thomson; Mr Peter Underwood; Mr Carl Watt, Byre Theatre, St Andrews; the librarians and staff at Aberdeen, Banchory, Elgin, Inverness, Orkney, Shetland and the National Library of Scotland (Reference Services).

FOREWORD

There is nothing quite like a spine-chilling ghost story to fire the imagination and surely there cannot be any true ghost stories more exciting than those reported in the land of Buchan, Burns, Scott and Bonnie Prince Charlie.

There is far too much nonsense talked and written today about ghosts and haunted houses and far too few intelligent, practical and sensible books on the subject written by someone with an open mind who speaks from experience. We are fortunate indeed in having Norman Adams to chronicle the fascinating story of haunted Scotland.

Nearly 100 years ago the Italian investigator Cesare Lombroso stated: 'Note this well – that however doubtful each separate case may appear, in the ensemble they form such a compact web of proof as wholly to baffle the scalpel of doubt.' It is still true today. Taken individually almost any case of alleged haunting might be dismissed as hallucination, malobservation, trickery of some kind, or downright falsehood but taken collectively from all parts of the world, in all civilisations, by all kinds of people, since the beginning of recorded history, the evidence for ghosts and ghostly activity is completely overwhelming.

At no time, it would seem, has there been so much serious enquiry into the paranormal.

While there is still the regrettable spectacle on television and stage of what purports to be paranormal activity (in actual fact one of the few certainties of paranormal activity is its refusal or inability to perform on request) and this is one of the reasons that for some time now The Ghost Club Society has been collecting authentic ghost evidence. When it is felt that sufficient material has been accumulated it is planned to publish the whole mass of overwhelming evidence for paranormal activity, evidence that comes from different people, at different places and at different times, presenting an enormous and important presentation of evidence which will, we feel, be indisputable.

It was the Scot Andrew Lang who said that most of the people who had seen ghosts were not highly imaginative and hysteric but 'steady, unimaginative, unexcitable persons who had just the one odd experience' that they simply could not explain. I have not only enjoyed this book and learned from it but my own study of such happenings enables me to condone many of the author's facts. Indeed I am acquainted with some of the cases he explores and records with such enthusiasm, knowledge and sincerity.

Stories of true ghostly happenings often suffer, it has to be admitted, from their seldom being first hand. All too often the happenings are related by someone who heard them from someone who had learned of the matter from someone else. Here the author, whose previous works on the subject have been well received, personally visits haunted properties and personally talks with people immediately concerned. He is to be congratulated on his objectivity.

What is quite certain in these difficult regions is that sooner or later we encounter the problem of what has been described as 'the undoubted queerness of time'.

Time is not the simple one-way street we tend to assume it is. If and when we solve the problem of time we may well be on the way to solving the problems of many ghostly appearances.

Peter Underwood, FRSA,
President of The Ghost Club Society

INTRODUCTION

In search of Scottish ghosts I have recorded cases from the northernmost, rock-girt Shetland Islands to the green, rounded landscape of the Borders.

My quest took me to a gleaming supermarket, bursting with life, yet reputedly haunted, in the cathedral city of Elgin, and a hidden corner of Old Edinburgh, where I left a propitiatory gift for the sad wraith of a little girl, who is said to welcome visitors to her murky world.

I dogged the footsteps of controversial Victorian ghosthunter Ada Goodrich Freer and her fellow investigators exactly 100 years after they set out to solve the mysteries of Ballechin House, Scotland's answer to Borley Rectory – 'the most haunted house in England'.

Scotland is a land of ghosts and haunted places. It abounds with stories of haunted castles, houses, roads, battlefields, hotels, pubs, theatres and mountains. Ghosts, it seems, get everywhere. They've also been reported in schools, colleges and factories. A snooker club in Glasgow has a spook. I spoke to an oilman who claimed a ghostly experience on a North Sea oil rig.

Phantoms are as likely to sport yachting clothes, as worn by the aforementioned oil rig entities, and flying gear favoured by the Montrose Aerodrome ghost, as the vestments of a spectral monk or the armour of the Black Knight of Rosslyn. But whatever the nature of the haunting I found it was the frightening experiences of ordinary folk which caused my spine to tingle. I hope you agree.

Norman Adams
Banchory 1998

CHAPTER 1

THE UNINVITED

You don't have to live in an ancestral castle or a grand mansion to be haunted. Ghosts are equally at home in a private flat with all mod cons, a country cottage or council property.

The Cameron family live in Thornhill, a trim council house estate on the fringe of the Morayshire town of Forres. Their home is in a row of houses, each with a small front garden protected by a wooden fence. The back door faces a drying green and communal square. But there is one difference. Their home attracted an uninvited guest!

Mother of four, Livonia Cameron, and her Merchant Navy husband Jim have lived happily in the comfortable, two-floored house for 17 years. On the ground floor there is a front parlour and kitchen, while upstairs accommodation consists of three bedrooms and a bathroom.

When I interviewed the family, Mr Cameron was at sea and only their son, Christopher, who is in his mid-20s, stayed at home with his mum. His parents' room is at the front of the house, and Chris slept in the back bedroom, its walls decorated with bright posters. His younger brother James and two sisters, Suzie and Angela, lived elsewhere in Forres. It was Suzie, who is in her late 20s, who wrote to me about the strange phenomena which took place at the family home.

The Camerons experienced everything from phantom footsteps,

rapping and disembodied voices to hair-tugging and the frightening appearance of a caped figure resembling a photo negative.

The Cameron household was a picture of domesticity when I called. The two cats, Pepi and Sooty, were demanding my attention and ignoring the caged canary. The stairway wall was adorned with souvenirs of Jim Cameron's voyages around the world.

Mrs Cameron described how a tap on her shoulder in the kitchen heralded the arrival of the entity, if entity it was. In time this was followed by the sound of the back door being opened and shut even though the door was locked. While in bed she heard footsteps mounting the stairs and halt at her bedroom door which was open at the time. There was no one there. 'That really put the wind up me,' she confessed.

She saw her uninvited guest in January 1995 when she turned in for the night. She closed her book and switched off her bedside lamp. Chris was asleep in his room at the end of the hallway, next to the bathroom. The first indication that something was wrong was when Sooty, who was in Mrs Cameron's bed, began yowling.

'I was facing my bedroom door, which was open, and could see along the hallway to the door of Chris's bedroom,' she explained. 'The next thing a figure appeared at the top of the stairs. It was misty grey and human shaped, and appeared to be wearing a cloak. It was facing Chris's room. I thought I was seeing things so I blinked twice but the figure was still there. I thought it peculiar but I felt no fear.'

Mrs Cameron decided not to tell the rest of the family. But a few days later when James and his girlfriend visited the house the girl was startled when a figure vanished through a wall cupboard. Her description of the sinister figure matched that of the apparition seen by Mrs Cameron.

A few months later Mrs Cameron spent a sleepless night after another frightening experience. As she lay with her head on the pillow her hair was twice tugged from behind. 'When my hair was pulled the second time I felt my head going back,' she explained.

Although both Angela and Suzie attracted the entity – Angie felt an unseen hand press the small of her back while Suzie was tapped on the shoulder while home alone feeding the cats – the most terrifying encounter was experienced by Chris.

In the winter of 1995 he was endeavouring to fall asleep when he heard the sound of hollow laughter. His bedroom was illuminated by the glow of street lamps and the hallway light shining under the gap of his closed door. He felt his blood turn to ice when he saw a tall, black figure standing in front of the door. 'I tried to scream for help but couldn't,' he said. 'I seemed pinned to my bed and it was only when it approached that I was able to scramble out of bed. By that time it had vanished.

'I did not make out any features – not its face, hands or legs. It appeared to be wearing something black and flowing. I sat shocked on the edge of the bed. I did not mention what I had seen until much later that day.'

Chris firmly denied my suggestion that he had been in a grip of a nightmare. The family contacted a minister and later called in a medium who gave Mrs Cameron instructions on how to carry out a 'psychic cleansing'. She left Mrs Cameron a bottle of solvent with instructions to wipe carefully the walls of her home but to avoid physically touching them. A candle was burned in each room during the ritual, and the entity told in no uncertain manner who slept in the rooms. 'After the visit we felt more relaxed,' said Suzie. Everything quietened down until a few days later when Mrs Cameron awoke at 1 a.m. on hearing her name called. The strange thing is that when her husband was home on leave nothing happened.

Thornhill was built on farmland, part of which was a prisoner-of-war camp during the Second World War.

But although the entity may have quit the Cameron household Mrs Cameron saw something strange outside her home on 10 February 1996. After putting Pepi outside she stared out of her kitchen window as a black shapeless thing drifted past her home. 'It was moving behind the hedge and seemed to walk through our neighbours' parked car. It made my hair stand on end.'

Oddly enough, in April 1996 two women neighbours living across from the Camerons told her of being roused from their sleep by mysterious rapping and knocking on the walls of their homes.

As I left the Cameron household my attention was drawn to a sticker: 'May peace prevail on earth.' Amen to that!

In May 1993 a young bachelor moved into a one-bedroomed council house on the top floor of a block of flats in the Sinclairtown district of Kirkcaldy, Fife. Seven months later Mark Anderson, who is in his 20s, was preparing to make a hasty departure after claiming his home was haunted.

Phantom footfalls, tapping noises, the ringing of a handbell, cold spots and a misty faceless apparition at the foot of his bed, gave him sleepless nights. Mark's claim was supported by a former tenant who had spent five years in the same flat. Mark had no intention of staying as long as the previous householder and asked the local housing authority for an exchange.

The case attracted considerable media publicity, and within a few days Mark was visited by two psychic investigators, one of whom declared on breakfast time television that the flat was haunted by not one, but five spectres, identifying them as three men, an old woman and a white-cloaked figure. After Mark quit the flat he enlisted the support of a local councillor. There was talk of holding an exorcism, but nothing came of that.

The flat in Sutherland Place was visited by another woman ghosthunter and she suggested that one of the two non-paying residents was Mark's grandfather, who had been dead for two years. The old man got the blame for fiddling with the electrical fittings to let his grandson know he was around. When I spoke to Mark he confirmed the alleged haunting and described how at 4.20 a.m. his ghetto-blaster suddenly came to life, although it was switched off at the mains. Electrical appliances seem to hold an attraction for ghosts. In Mark's flat they also delighted in making objects, including a box of teabags and toenail clippers, vanish into thin air.

Mark returned to his flat and he was still there when I spoke to him. He claimed he still saw figures move around his bedroom, but as they seemed 'friendly' he had no wish to get rid of them. So far.

Haunted council flats are not uncommon in Kirkcaldy. In the space of 14 years two families in the same street quit their homes after supernatural occurrences. One family was rehoused after their Member of Parliament spent a night alone in their haunted home.

Paranormal activity in a house can sometimes be traced back to a time before the dwelling was erected. That's why a ghosthunter roots out the history of a property and the land on which it stands to see if it harbours a clue to the haunting.

But psychic investigators who knocked on the door of a new council house in Airdrie, Lanarkshire, were taken aback by an uninvited tenant's reason for being there. The married couple who occupied the house had returned home one night to find the apparition of an old lady standing beside the ornamental stone fireplace. The couple were scared out of their wits and consulted the Scottish Society for Psychical Research. The case was investigated by the society's president, Professor Archie Roy, and a well-known Glasgow medium and healer, Albert Best, now deceased.

The couple were the first tenants and the history of the surrounding land proved uninspiring. However, it emerged that the couple had built the fireplace with stones they had recovered from a derelict house. Unknown to them they had 'adopted' the earthbound ghost of the lady who had previously lived in the house. The lady believed she was still alive and well in her own home, which had been reduced to a pile of stones on the other side of the town.

The heading of this chapter is 'The Uninvited', alluding to the resident ghost. But when I visit a haunted house I sometimes ask myself who are the 'uninvited'? Is it really the current occupier? An American in Scotland experienced several shocking encounters with the ghost of a former resident when he leased an 18th-century cottage in the Angus countryside.

In December 1992, three months after John moved in, he was

awakened around 9 a.m. on a Sunday by what felt like a pair of hands gripping his waist. He was lying on his right-hand side and the entity was trying to roll him on to his back. He sensed an old woman was responsible. He seemed paralysed and unable to resist the efforts to roll him on to his back. But once he was rolled flat on his back the bed began to shake for approximately 30 seconds. After about five minutes the bed shook again for several seconds.

In January 1993 the 43-year-old bachelor stood inside his front door beside the telephone. He was looking up a number in the phone book. It was around five in the evening and it was dark outside. Suddenly there were four or five distinctive raps on the door and he immediately opened it. An overhead light showed there was no one there. He checked the nearby lane but he was alone.

The following month John and some Scottish friends held an evening of traditional Scots and Irish music, and some guests slept over. The host and three other men slept in a room upstairs and the ladies occupied another room. At 8 a.m. the next day John's bed began to shake but he did not tell his guests, thinking they would ridicule him.

John, who has lived in Scotland for eight years, moved from the West Coast to the Montrose area. His home is a former coachman's house which is near an older building built by an old Angus family. On a day trip to Montrose John had a chance encounter with a woman who had knowledge of the haunting. She told him the great house and former coachman's cottage were reputed to have a female 'presence', and that the last surviving member of the landowning family to live in the cottage was a spinster who had died at the turn of the century.

However, the ghost had already been seen in John's cottage by a woman guest. She had got up to make breakfast, and was about to switch on the television, when she saw the apparition sitting in a rocking-chair. The chair is real enough. It is a colonial rocking-chair bought in New York State and gifted to John by his sister. The ghost was of a woman in her 50s or 60s. She was wearing a brown dress and white apron in the style of the late 19th century. The guest was startled and screamed in fright.

In August 1996 John had a disturbing experience after returning from a trip to the West Coast late on a Sunday night. He was no sooner in the house when he heard scratching from behind a wall. He thought it might be caused by a mouse or a trapped bird. At 2.20 a.m. on the Monday he was wakened by 'very loud footsteps' climbing the stairs. The footfalls continued into the bathroom before stopping. He had a strong feeling of evil and began to perspire. He was too frightened to investigate and lay with the light on for half an hour in mounting apprehension. At 3.20 a.m. shoes and other items in a wall cupboard in his bedroom began to 'toss around'. Not surprisingly he did not get out of bed to investigate. The scratching noise in the wall resumed. Later that morning he inspected the wall cupboard and found nothing out of place. He described the occurrences of that night as 'ominous'. For several nights following this episode he took a heavy stick to bed with him, but the phenomena ceased.

Said John: 'Before I came to Scotland I was completely sceptical about ghosts and the paranormal. Today I am convinced such phenomena exist.'

Why did the ghost single out the new tenant?

'Perhaps merely to assert its presence or to protest and display annoyance that I was occupying its former home,' added John. 'However, there is really no clear way of knowing – it's all just a curious mystery that may never be explained.'

A ghost dubbed 'Jane' caused the owners of a Victorian house in the west end of Aberdeen a few sleepless nights. Many of the weird disturbances, including hideous screams, took place around the time the house became occupied after being converted into luxury flats.

My footsteps echoed around the mosaic-floored front hall when I visited the house in the King's Gate area. It was here my host caught a brief glimpse of the resident ghost, and it was from the hall that the blood-chilling cries rang out.

Walter, a city businessman, detected something strange about his first-floor flat when he was given the keys in January 1990. He took a colleague to see his new acquisition but as they inspected the rooms she complained of a smell in the bedroom. Walter told me: 'I can only describe it as a deathly smell. It was a heavy, strange odour that seemed to waft past our noses. I changed the carpet but the smell occasionally returned, and there have been times since when I have detected it in the bedroom.'

Walter moved into his new home the following month. He had been busy during the preceding weeks decorating and on his first night he ran a bath. He put on a Carpenters' number on his hi-fi in the lounge, and relaxed in the tub. 'All of a sudden the hi-fi was blaring,' added Walter. 'The music was so loud it was distorted. It was at full blast.' Wrapping a towel around his waist he dashed into the room to turn down the volume.

'My first thought was for my new neighbours,' he said. 'I got within a few feet of the hi-fi when I clearly saw the dial turn on its own accord until the sound faded. It has never done that since. I checked the machine. It was not faulty.'

The next morning, a Monday, Walter left home. He was heading for the bank. He went down to the ground floor and was about to unlock the main front door when he realised he had left his bank card in his flat. He turned to hurry back upstairs, but as he spun on his heel he saw the solid figure of a woman. She was standing at a dark oak dresser, which belonged to neighbours, and was situated at the foot of the stairs. The dresser existed, but the woman did not. Walter snapped his fingers at me. 'She vanished like that.'

The woman, whom he took to be in her late 20s or early 30s, had her back to him. She appeared to be polishing the top of the dresser. The woman was wearing a dark, ankle-length dress of heavy material with knee-length, flouncy material. It reminded Walter of a character from the television series, *Upstairs, Downstairs*.

'A shiver ran down my back but I did not think I had seen a

ghost,' said Walter. He never again saw the apparition, but the uncanny disturbances did not abate.

In 1994 Walter went to bed before midnight. He had a guest, his chum, Ross, who slept in a folding bed in the lounge. He was recapping the day's events at work in his head when a terrible scream shattered his reverie. It was a woman's scream and it seemed to begin in the hallway below and rise to the ornamental roof at the top of the house. He and Ross dashed out of the flat and peered into the empty stair-well. Walter also checked the darkened street from the window of his flat, but it was deserted. Walter described the cry as 'an old scream, the sort you hear in a black and white movie. After that incident I thought there was something in the house.'

Strange incidents began happening in Walter's flat. A wall clock frequently stopped (and still does) before the bewitching hour, although a clockmaker could find no fault. Mysterious smudges appeared on his carpet and on occasions he has experienced a 'cold spot', that is a drop in temperature indicating heat loss in the area of a haunting.

But the mystery deepened the evening Walter came home from work and sank gratefully into an armchair and switched on the television. His startled gaze fell on an ornament which stood on top of a Chinese chest of drawers. The single ornament featured two, 15-inch-high figures of nuns. The expensive ornament was in place but the nuns' heads had been neatly lopped off and placed at its base. Walter was astounded. He was the only occupant of the flat. He did not employ a cleaner and no one else had a door key. I examined the statuettes and I can attest to the neatness of the decapitations. So much for the ghost being house-proud!

Walter's neighbour, Sue, was able to throw fresh light on the haunting. Sue, who lives directly above, bought her flat at least a year before Walter. She supported Walter's account of the scream in the night. 'It was horrible,' she said. 'It definitely was a woman's voice. I just had to come out and see what was happening.' A third person — there are five flats in the house — commented on the scream to Sue later that day. But it was not the first time Sue had been startled by a woman screaming in the hall. 'The first time I heard a scream was before Walter moved in. I thought I was imagining things. It happened in the early hours and it reminded me of somebody being forcibly removed from the building. At the time I presumed it was horseplay, but I did not check on the cause.'

Although Sue has never seen an apparition it was she who dubbed the ghost 'Jane'. Sue's flat has not escaped the ghost's attention. While sitting talking with a male friend one night they saw a glass candlestick suddenly take off from the top of the television set. 'It did not fall,' she explained. 'It went up in the air and shattered in two places. Half of the candlestick, the base unit, ended up beside the stereo, two feet away. About an inch and a half in the middle of the candlestick had shattered into tiny pieces, but the rest was untouched. It was as though someone had given it a karate chop.'

When Sue owned a cat its favourite plaything was a ping-pong ball. The animal would fish the ball out of a glass dish and bat it around the floor. She no longer has the pet but someone is still playing tricks with the ball. One time the ball had been removed from the deep-shaped bowl and left on the carpet. On another occasion the ball vanished from her sight and mind for days until it turned up on the lounge floor.

Sue struck me as a strong-willed young lady. This was borne out by her actions one night when she was disturbed by the continual banging of the street door. She left her upstairs flat and checked on the door. She described how she stood within a few feet of the door, listening to it banging, although it did not move an inch. It was not the first time this had happened. 'I know there is something here, but things have settled,' she went on. 'It's a nice house. "Jane" seems to have accepted us and has settled down.'

Who was 'Jane'? Since the house was built in the 19th century the previous owners have included ministers, advocates and military men, although one spinster lady lived there for at least quarter of a century. It might be pure speculation to claim it is her ghost that haunts the flats, for in its heyday such a big house employed a great number of domestic staff.

Before I left Walter he told me a creepy story concerning a neighbouring house. As soon as he moved in he was aware of an elderly woman staring at him from an upstairs window. She never seemed to leave her post at night. She got on his nerves so much he was reduced to drawing his curtains whenever he spotted her. He learned much later that the room was supposed to be haunted by the ghost of an old lady.

After the Argo family moved into one of the oldest houses in the Spital, the ancient narrow thoroughfare that links Old Aberdeen with Aberdeen, strange things began to occur. John Argo was a self-employed baker in those days, with his bakehouse in the back garden and the shop on the ground floor. In the winter of 1966 he and his wife Moyra were relaxing in their living-room when heavy footsteps were heard on the stairs leading to the bedrooms. The descending footfalls halted at the living-room door. Suspecting one of their four children was out of bed, John hurried to the door. He found the hallway empty and a quick check revealed that their three sons and daughter were fast asleep.

The mysterious thumps and noises continued over the next few weeks. They were heard in the bakehouse where John's part-time assistant refused to work alone at night. The couple were entertaining a woman friend when their conversation was interrupted by three loud thumps on the front door. Needless to say there was no caller.

The family Labrador dog began acting oddly, then a ghost made an appearance while the Argos slept in a bed settee in the living-room. John wakened to see a strange man with a dog materialise from a wall cupboard. The man was short and fat, hatless, and wore a gabardine coat tied with a bit of twine round the waist. He was accompanied by a black and white dog on a string lead. Said Mr Argo: 'The man and dog were both solid looking but when they reached halfway across the room they vanished. I did not waken my wife but told her later.'

It was only recently that the Argos learned of the identity of the ghost. In the course of conversation with a former resident the ghost story was mentioned. 'Oh, that's Mr Alexander!' said the woman. 'He used to live next door.' Mr Alexander's home was demolished and the rebuilding work probably brought about the haunting.

Although things have quietened down, Mr Argo, a taxi driver, believes there is still a ghost afoot. When he finishes work in the early hours he claims he sometimes hears soft music in the kitchen, although the radio and portable television are both switched off. Yet another example perhaps of how electrical gadgets fascinate ghosts.

Two doors up from the Argos the wraith of a Victorian lady in grey clutching a bunch of keys was reported 20 years ago in an 18th-century building once used as a house of correction for vice girls. The ghost is believed to have been that of the matron. Inmates of the Aberdeen Female Penitentiary, now a private residence, earned their keep mending clothes and taking in laundry.

One man and his dog might have returned to haunt the Argo household after his old home was demolished. But what or who was behind the frightening ordeal of a Caithness couple on a week-end break at relatives in rural Aberdeenshire?

In 1980 Fiona and James Campbell stayed at a farm cottage in the parish of Kinellar, near Kintore. In the early hours of a fine, clear day they were wakened by the whimpering of their hosts' pet collie in the adjoining kitchen. A dragging sound and heavy footsteps came from the back of the house. The sound drew closer, and eventually they saw the black figure of a man through the window. He was bent double and walking backwards as if he was dragging something heavy.

The couple talked in whispers as the figure moved past their vantage point. It stooped over its load, paused, then continued dragging the unseen burden along the ground. To their horror the figure walked straight through the sun-porch as if it was not there.

'I cannot begin to describe our fear,' Fiona told me. 'It wasn't anything we had ever experienced before. Shortly after, the noise faded and the dog settled down.' The couple were unable to get a satisfactory explanation from their hosts. 'We are convinced we saw a ghost. Never before or since have either of us felt the same cold fear.'

Retired art teacher Bill Smith recounted an equally scary experience in his studio while studying in Edinburgh.

The studio, a timber and corrugated structure, had been a former dispensary operated by nuns at St David's Roman Catholic Convent, near Dublin Street, in the New Town. Everybody who visited the studio found it an attractive place with a peaceful and pleasant atmosphere, even during the ghostly episodes which were witnessed by Mr Smith and his student friends at Edinburgh College of Art.

A variety of objects and pieces of furniture were moved from one spot to the other, and the external door to the studio garden, which adjoined the convent garden, was repeatedly opened and shut violently. 'It was a very angry sound,' recalled Mr Smith. A partition prevented him or his friends from seeing whether the door actually moved on these occasions, but the door was locked at all times. One day Bill and two students saw a sheet of brown paper suddenly rise vertically into the air from the floor. There was no hint of a draught of air.

Events in the tiny studio became a topic of conversation and whenever Mr Smith and his friends walked into the local pub they were asked: 'What's the ghost doing today?'

But the laughter faded when Mr Smith awoke around 3 a.m., his heart racing madly. A woman's disembodied voice, filled with despair, rang out: 'Oh, no! Oh, no! Oh, no!' That night he shared the studio with two mates, one of whom had been evicted from his digs. He occupied a camp bed. Mr Smith had his own bed, while the remaining student slept on a divan. The man in the camp bed was 'terrified out of his wits' by the eerie voice. None of the three men saw a woman and for the next few nights the terrified student slept with a flashlight on. 'We were all affected emotionally by what had taken place,' said Mr Smith, who now lives in Morayshire.

He was unable to get to the bottom of the mystery. After consulting the convent nuns – they belonged to the Order of the Helpers of the Holy Souls – he was put in touch with a priest. He gave Mr Smith a glass phial containing holy water and a medallion inscribed with a prayer and instructed him to sprinkle his studio with the water while repeating the prayer. Mr Smith, who is not a Catholic, performed this act, and later slept with the phial under his pillow. He was told if the disturbances continued an exorcism would be performed. This was not necessary for there was no further trouble.

About eight years ago Mr Smith returned to Edinburgh to see his old studio torn down. During the visit he heard a macabre ghost story linked with a nearby house. He was told of a couple who lived in a basement flat who were frightened by ghostly disturbances, not unlike those which plagued Mr Smith's studio almost 40 years ago. An occupant was disturbed from his sleep by a man in a stovepipe hat at the foot of his bed.

It seems the house had belonged to a doctor whose daughter had vanished at play. Her tragic father was driven insane by her disappearance and spent every available moment searching for her. Years later, Mr Smith was told, workmen carrying out alterations in the house came across a child's skeleton trapped in a flue.

There was no mention of a child's ghost haunting the house but, sadly, I have come across several hauntings by ghost children. In another Edinburgh district, Trinity, I spoke to the occupant of an old house which is haunted by the ghost of a little girl. Her apparition has been seen and there have also been reports of disembodied voices and the sound of a bouncing ball as though the ghost was at play. Her identity is not known.

As soon as a young woman moved into her new luxury flat in a converted textile mill in Tillicoultry, near Stirling, in October 1993, she felt she was not alone. 'I had an unaccountable and horrible feeling of being watched,' she told me.

But Fiona (that is her middle name) did not know by whom or what. 'Whenever I had the feeling of being watched I would grow really cold. But I dismissed it as imagination, even when I entered the bathroom one morning and found the bath and tiled walls smeared with shower gel sprayed from a pump dispenser. There was no rational explanation as I was alone and nobody else had access to my flat. I put the incident to the back of my mind.'

Fiona had hung a car air-freshener on the handle of the living-room door. Whenever she returned to the room she found it lying in the centre of the room. There was no question that the freshener had been blown off by a sudden draught. Even so she carried out a number of experiments with the door – swinging it back and forth violently or banging it shut because Fiona has a dread of spiders and insisted on keeping the windows of her flat firmly shut. But the freshener either remained in place on the door handle or dropped at her feet.

Fiona admitted: 'At this stage I was really getting nervous and I was beginning to wonder if there was a ghost, or if I was going out of my mind.' But the disturbances increased. One evening as Fiona turned her attention to the hi-fi in the living-room she was distinctly aware of someone running past her. She felt a rush of cold air and footfalls. 'I spun round to see who it was. I really thought there was an intruder in my flat but there was nobody there. I was absolutely paralysed with fear.' Slowly, Fiona sank to the floor with her back pressed against the wall. She was struck dumb and for half an hour she remained seated, her eyes darting around the room. She had the uncontrollable urge to flee the flat but eventually managed to calm her frayed nerves.

Fiona confided in a neighbour and some friends but they laughed off the incidents and even went to the length of playing silly pranks when visiting her.

'Some nights I would arrive home in the evening and everything would be fine,' said Fiona. 'But there were times when I knew something was about to happen. I could feel the hairs on the back of my neck begin to rise.'

Her most frightening experience took place one night as she slept. 'All of a sudden there was the thundering of feet as if someone was running in a circle in the middle of my bedroom. I tried to swing my legs over the edge of my bed but I couldn't move a muscle. I was absolutely petrified. I tried to scream or call out but could not find my voice.'

The running footsteps lasted five minutes or so but seemed like an eternity.

Fiona started spending weekends with her parents, returning to Tillicoultry with a feeling of dread. The disturbances manifested themselves in other ways. She called in engineers after the storage heaters played up. An engineer told her the electric meter had been tampered with yet the seal was unbroken.

Fiona also found scribble marks on a wall. They appeared to have been made by a crayon but were unreadable. Elsewhere in the flat a wall was covered with 'gunge' which did not come from any container in the flat.

Unknown to Fiona she was given a clue to who was responsible for the psychic phenomena. Before turning in one evening she experienced the tell-tale signs of an imminent haunting. The hairs on the nape of her neck bristled. 'I tried to put this fear to the back of my mind and decided to retire to bed. I gathered up the cups from the living-room and was about to put the lights out when I noticed some strange marks on one of the mirrors that stood beside the door.' On closer inspection Fiona saw what appeared to be two very sticky handprints and a couple of smears. 'The prints seemed perfectly formed,' said Fiona. 'I placed my own hand over the top of them to gauge their size and they were about half the size of mine and obviously belonged to a child. Nobody smaller than myself had been in the flat. I racked my brain for a rational solution but could not find one.'

Fiona was again disturbed from her sleep when she was suddenly aware of a heavy force pressing down on the foot of her bed as if someone had clambered on to it.

Fiona sought help from two mediums, both women, who visited

her in an attempt to make contact with the entity that had upset her life. On their visit Fiona learned that the flat was haunted by a little, blond-haired boy of four or five years old. In fact, one of the mediums claimed she could see the child standing in the carpark below the block of flats!

Fiona found the revelation comforting. 'I had visions that my home was haunted by a horrible old man.' A medium identified the ghost boy as 'Peter'. 'They did not throw any light on who he was but explained he had come to me as he felt safe and secure as he sensed I had a love of children.'

But how do you deal with a mischievous little ghost? 'I was told to treat him like any normal child. When he became naughty I was to tell him to stop.' There was no question of Fiona threatening corporal punishment.

Fiona was determined to establish the identity of 'Peter', or 'Little Tommy', as he was dubbed by some of her friends. While checking the files of the *Alloa Advertiser* she discovered that a local child had drowned in an ornamental pond at the mill in the summer of 1963. But the two-year-old victim was a girl! However, Fiona accepts the medium's findings that the ghost is of a little boy.

By the end of 1994 things at the flat had quietened down, but not once did the owner catch a glimpse of her uninvited guest. She also learned that before moving into the block of flats some strange occurrences had taken place in the area of her flat. Packed lunches brought by workers mysteriously vanished and a painter, who had been working alone in the flat, returned to be met by a stack of planks clattering down the stairs towards him.

If we accept that 'Peter' haunted the flat, who was he? In Victorian times child labour was exploited by industrialists. While most youngsters employed in mills started at the age of eight, a boy of Peter's tender years might have met with a fatal accident while accompanying his family to their workplace. But that is pure speculation.

A ghost child who plagued a house in Aberdeen's Osborne Place in the 1970s was given its marching orders by the owner. Everyday objects, such as a pen and cushions, were flung around a room to the annoyance of the man of the house. Determined to get to the bottom of the haunting he did some research and discovered that a little girl had died in the house in the 19th century. The next time a pen leapt into the air he chastised the ghost by name and ordered her to stop the horseplay. He had no further trouble.

But imagine the reaction of a housewife who found a ghost boy in her larder. The woman in question lived in an old farmhouse at Drumoak, Aberdeenshire, and it was there she was confronted by the poignant figure of a small boy in blue. He was aged about 12 and wore an anxious expression on his pale countenance, as if, the woman told me, 'he wanted to communicate with me'. But each time the ghost drifted across the floor towards her it vanished. She saw it countless times and never once felt afraid. Even her son saw the unhappy little ghost.

The woman made some discreet inquiries and was told that the boy had died violently and was buried in the graveyard at Dalmaik Kirk, a picturesque ruin on the north bank of the River Dee.

There is no doubt about who is the 'uninvited' in one of the strangest hauntings in present-day Scotland. It concerns a middle-aged couple who picknicked in a Borders beauty spot in the summer of 1996.

Afterwards the husband and wife made the return trip on foot to their home a few miles away. The wife suddenly realised they were being accompanied by a little girl, aged about ten, wearing a dress from the days of the Covenanters. The apparition, which was invisible to her husband, attached itself to the terrified wife, and accompanied the couple to their home. As far as I know the ghost girl is still there.

A short distance off the Glens of Foudland stretch of the busy Aberdeen to Inverness road is a haunted cottage, where, on two nights during a nine-month let, a young married couple were shocked by the supernatural.

The first strange incident took place in January 1992 when the couple returned late one Sunday night from a weekend jaunt in

Glasgow. Before departing on the Friday they had prepared the fire in the living-room. Kindling and paper were in place, but no paraffin was used.

They did not light the fire on their return but settled down on the sofa with steaming bowls of broth. Suddenly, the fire lit itself! The husband told me: 'I swear the fire burst into flames without a match. The grate was stone cold when we left for Glasgow. We were absolutely amazed, but it really did not hit us until the next morning.'

A few nights later a storm battered the darkened cottage as the husband drove home from his office in Aberdeen. His wife was still at work. Yet the front door of the house was wide open to the howling elements. The man kept the engine of his car running as he suspected burglars and was ready to make a quick getaway. Warily he entered the cottage and switched on lights. Everything seemed untouched except for the chiming clock, which had never worked since they took over the tenancy. Now the old clock was ticking away on the mantelpiece with the hands pointing at the correct time!

Had a former resident returned from the grave to check on the new occupants?

I asked the same question after Aberdeen author George Gordon told me of a remarkable demonstration of the paranormal at the farmhouse of Graystonefaulds, which stands in the parish of Glass, near Huntly, Aberdeenshire.

Mr Gordon, who was born and educated in Glass, knew Graystonefaulds well as a boy. Many a call did he and his Aunt Mary make on the farmer Jimmy Gauld, who figures in the subsequent ghost story, and his wife Jane. Mr Gordon remembers him as a nice friendly man who would sit in his chair by the fireside quietly smoking his pipe, with an occasional spit into a makeshift spittoon – a box of sawdust.

When his wife died in 1922 Jimmy Gauld was approaching 70 years of age. A close relative of his late wife, George Duncan came to live at Graystonefaulds with his wife, Mary, and family. Jimmy was glad of the company and the Duncans settled in right fine. But in 1923 for some unaccountable reason Jimmy Gauld decided to emigrate to Toronto, Canada, to spend the remainder of his life with his son Tom. He corresponded with the Duncans and he seemed to be settling down quite happily.

At Graystonefaulds, on the night of 12 December 1924, the Duncans had great difficulty in falling sleep. George Gordon explained why. 'Not long after retiring, lying awake after a fitful sleep, both heard movement in the house, the sound of someone walking across the floor downstairs, and then the same footsteps in a bedroom upstairs.'

The Duncans were alarmed. They checked the time. It was 1.10 a.m. Mr Duncan called out, but there was no answer. He then rose to examine the locks and search the downstairs rooms, but all were secure and nothing amiss. Mystified and not a little disturbed they concluded that the steps seemed to resemble those of old Jimmy Gauld, just as though he were walking about as they heard him do in the recent past. But Jimmy was in Canada thousands of miles away. Or was he?

The Duncans had three daughters, but on questioning them next day they had been fast asleep and had heard nothing.

The mystery remained until a letter arrived from Jimmy's son informing the Duncans that his father had died on 13 December at exactly the same time as the couple had been disturbed by the phantom footsteps!

CHAPTER 2

ROAD HAZARDS

The *Highway Code* does not include a road warning sign: 'Drive Carefully. Ghost Ahead!' But perhaps it should, for many of Scotland's roads are haunted.

Spectral stagecoaches, phantom motor cars and apparitions of all shapes and sizes have frightened and fascinated travellers.

The banshee, the ghost of a wailing woman who appears on the eve of a death in a family, is more associated with Irish folklore. But on a bright, moonlit night on 11 January 1797, a banshee stalked a road near the Banffshire town of Keith. Shortly before eight o'clock two men, both strangers, called at a farm before moving on along the country road.

Shortly afterwards an eerie wailing shattered the stillness. 'So loud and extraordinary was the sound that the people left their houses to see what it was that was passing,' wrote Reverend Walter Gordon in 1881. 'To the amazement of everyone nothing was to be seen, though it was moonlight, and moonlight so bright that it aroused attention.'

The weird keening chilled hearts, for all believed something terrible was about to happen. But even as they argued the cause flames blazed out on the nearby Hill of Auchinachie. The cottage of Cottertown was in flames and when the fire was extinguished the mangled bodies of 80-year-old George Milne and his daughter Meg were found. A blood-smeared axe lay nearby.

Robbery was the motive for a fat wallet was missing. Two shoe buckles belonging to the murderers were discarded in the struggle but, despite this vital clue and a reward of one hundred guineas for their arrest, they were never brought to justice.

In August 1809 Andrew Hossack was caught red-handed while robbing a cottage at Rubislaw in Aberdeen. While awaiting execution rumours swept the burgh that Hossack was implicated in the brutal murder. The accusation worried Hossack so much that he arranged for a minister to draw up a declaration of innocence which he read on the scaffold.

Brutal murder is woven into the story of a road phantom which was regularly seen near the Border village of St Boswells until the turn of this century. The apparition was said to be that of an elderly clergyman who murdered his housekeeper. The case was authenticated by the Society of Psychical Research although the story behind the haunting sounds untrustworthy. The ghost was described as a tall, pale-faced figure, wearing a black coat, with silk stockings, knee buckles, white cravat and a low-crowned black hat. It was seen about a dozen times, mostly by young women, with the last known appearance in August 1900.

In the autumn of 1975 supernatural road hazards were far from John Birnie's mind as he drove his family to a new life in Stornoway, where he was to take up a new job as manager of a savings bank. There were five people in the car. Mr Birnie was at the wheel, his eldest son, Russell, was in the front passenger seat, while in the back were his wife, Helen, and their two other youngsters, Owen and Linzi.

A light drizzle dampened the twilight as they travelled westwards on the A832 road between Muir of Ord and Gorstan in Ross-shire. Moments earlier they had passed through the hamlet of Garve.

Mr Birnie, who has now retired to Fochabers in Morayshire, described what happened next. 'Suddenly, the figure of a woman appeared in the middle of the road ahead, walking in our direction. She resembled a Victorian waitress. She was wearing a black uniform, with a white cap, and matching cuffs and waistband. Her head was bowed and she seemed to have her hands clasped in prayer.'

Mr Birnie took avoiding action but the woman seemed unperturbed by her narrow escape. Head down, and without a second glance, the figure strode purposefully towards Garve. 'The woman must have seen us for I had the sidelights on,' said Mr Birnie. 'Yet she took not a blind bit of notice. After we passed I looked in the rear mirror but there was no sign of her.'

Mrs Birnie corroborated her husband's story. 'It was definitely a waitress. She appeared to have on a little lace pinny, the sort of thing old-fashioned waitresses wore. But I cannot say if she had her hands clasped or not. I saw something, but whether it was a ghost or not I do not know. I have no other explanation for it.'

After passing the lone figure the Birnies crossed the Achnaclerach Bridge and continued on their journey to Ullapool to catch the ferry to Stornoway.

But the mystery of the Victorian waitress who appeared in the middle of a Highland road on a miserable October evening did not end there. In the early 1980s Mr Birnie was in a bus party that stopped at the Garve Hotel, and while being served he mentioned his strange encounter to a waitress. The hotel manager was interested to hear what Mr Birnie had to say. He had an equally astonishing story to pass on.

According to him, the ghost of a waitress in Victorian costume had often been seen on the stretch of road between the bridge and Garve. In life the woman had worked at the hotel, but had lodged at a nearby house, Hazelbrae. The poor woman became pregnant and had hurled herself off the bridge to drown in the Blackwater.

For more than quarter a century Ronald Macdonald Robertson travelled the countryside in search of Highland folktales. His version of the Garve ghost is different. He was told that the master of Hazelbrae had roused his wife's jealousy by showing too much affection to their maid. In a fit of revenge the mistress of the house placed some of her linen in the maid's trunk and then falsely accused the girl of theft. The girl denied the charge but the wife took her husband up to the maid's bedroom and opened the trunk containing the missing linen. The hapless girl threw her shawl over her head and ran from the house.

She threw herself into the river and her body was dragged from a pool at the back of Hazelbrae. Robertson made no mention of the girl being pregnant but he added an interesting footnote to the story. 'Since then the bells have rung periodically in that house, operated by no human agency. The usual time is the same hour at which the girl took her life.'

For more than 20 years John Hayton, a Lancashire man, and his wife, Patricia, and their family have lived in the district, and for 14 years they have lived at Hazelbrae. They had heard of the alleged haunting from local people, but they certainly have not heard any supernatural bell-ringing since they took up residence. Mrs Hayton kindly sent me an old postcard of Hazelbrae showing an angler fishing in the pool where the maid's body is reputed to have been found.

Cairnpapple is steeped in ancient mystery and magic. Its bleak, rounded summit, three miles north of the Lothian town of Bathgate, was sacred to early man, and on a clear day you can see why. The view from the hilltop is spectacular, extending from Goatfell on Arran in the west to the Firth of Forth in the east. On the summit Stone Age people erected a ring of upright stones, later used by Bronze and Iron Age man to construct tombs for cremated bodies and funeral pottery. No wonder it has been described as one of Scotland's most important prehistoric sites. But the Bathgate Hills conceal a baffling modern mystery – 'The Strange Case of the Silver Man'.

This being, entity or elemental, call it what you will, was encountered in the summer of 1988 on a forest road to the south-east of Cairnpapple by a family out for a late-night drive. At the wheel of the Fiesta was David Colman, father of three, and at the time a 33-year-old mature student. His front seat passenger was his wife Kathleen, while their two sons and a daughter, aged between six and 14, were in the back.

The strange encounter took place on a starry night on a road running parallel to Ravencraig Wood, popularly known as the Knock Forest, less than a mile from their home in Bathgate. The jaunt was unplanned, the youngsters having persuaded their father to take them for a ride in the new car.

As he headed for a small but steep incline topped with a dangerous right-hand bend, David's attention was instantly drawn to his right side. In a split second he saw a glowing figure, in classical running posture, moving extremely fast, possibly between 50 and 70 miles per hour! The figure was bulky and well over six feet tall. 'As it ran in the opposite direction from the car it had its head turned back towards us and appeared to be scowling,' David told me.

Silence gripped the occupants of the car. Then Kathleen asked her husband: 'You did see that, didn't you?' David replied: 'See what?' The children shouted in unison: 'You saw the silver man, daddy!'

Although the youngsters had unwittingly christened the bizarre creature, David said: 'The figure was white, not silver, but I suppose it appeared that way to the children. When I questioned them more closely they said the figure was crouched at the side of the road. As we approached it took off through the forest.'

Kathleen supported David's account. 'There was complete silence until I asked David if he had seen the figure,' she said. 'The expression on his face told it all.'

Kathleen, who saw the figure disappear into the forest, went on: 'It was a human shape, and I thought it was a male. I had a feeling it was not happy. It was not silver, more like a negative image. I remember the children were very excited.'

David, a registered staff nurse, claimed their previous home in Bathgate was haunted by phantom footsteps but that experience in no way compared with the night the Colmans came across the 'silver man' in the Bathgate Hills.

In the summer of 1973 or thereabouts the Scots television personality Phil Differ and a friend were driving back to Kilsyth in his Volkswagen Beetle when he saw a road phantom. Phil, who is known to television audiences as a writer, producer and presenter, was at the wheel while his companion was asleep in the front passenger's seat. In the glow of the vehicle's headlights Phil made out the hunched figure of an old woman walking at the side of the A803 road, between Banknock and Kilsyth. The woman had her back to the car and was trudging in the direction of Kilsyth, less than two miles away. Her clothes were blue-grey in colour and instead of shoes she had cloth wrapped around her feet. She was a huge woman and appeared to be lugging a pack.

Phil's angry response froze on his lips as the figure suddenly vanished. 'There was something old-fashioned about her,' Phil said. 'It was weird, and I got a terrible fright. It came to me later that I had probably seen a ghost.'

The identity of the ghost woman is unknown but had the phantom any connection with a bloody battle fought in the vicinity more than three centuries ago? She could have been one of the womenfolk whose partner fought at the Battle of Kilsyth in August 1645, when Montrose routed government troops.

Camp followers suffered terribly during the Scottish Civil Wars, and after Kilsyth Montrose's troops inflicted bloody revenge on government troops who had slaughtered their women at Methven, near Perth. Newark Castle in the Borders is reputed to be haunted by the ghosts of women and children camp followers murdered by Covenanters after Montrose was crushed at Philiphaugh.

A much-travelled spook is the phantom hitch-hiker, cases of which have been reported in all parts of the world. I refer to motorists who give lifts to supernatural travelling companions who then simply vanish before the end of their journey. In Scotland this strange phenomenon has taken a twist. Road users should be extra vigilant when travelling on roads around Aberdeen.

In November 1995 a city man claimed two terrifying close encounters with a white apparition while driving along busy Wellington Road, at the Loch of Loirston, just short of the main Aberdeen to Stonehaven dual carriageway.

In the first encounter he felt a thud as his car struck the figure, but a check revealed nothing untoward. A few months later the same figure vanished on impact but the driver was gripped by an icy cold atmosphere as if a 'presence' had entered the car. He quickly abandoned the vehicle and it was several minutes before he plucked up courage enough to slide back behind the driving wheel.

The same man claimed his mother ran into the figure while driving past the loch, but this time the road phantom seemed to go straight through the car windscreen before vanishing.

A motorist was passing through Stonehaven in the winter of 1995 when a phantom in a red cloak, resembling Red Riding Hood's apparel, crossed his path. 'I braked as I thought I might have knocked someone down,' he said, 'but there was nothing there. It was spooky and I was quite scared.'

I spoke to a couple who had a similar unpleasant experience while motoring in Fife in the 1960s. They were on the St Andrews to Cupar road on a bright moonlit night when the husband had the eerie feeling that 'two moons' were keeping pace with the car. There was a moon out, but what had caused the illusion of a second moon? Without warning an old man appeared in front of their car. 'I ran smack into the figure but there was no sound of a collision,' said the man, who admitted the memory still sent shivers up his spine. 'I leapt out and searched all around the car – I even looked under it – but there was no body.'

Road phantoms have been reported in other parts of Fife, and the Leven-based newspaper, *East Fife Mail,* has collected a dossier on mystery sightings.

One night in January 1997 a Methil man was driving on the Leven to Kennoway road when a figure garbed in black staggered drunkenly into the path of his car, then vanished. He informed the newspaper after reading an account of alleged sightings on the same road of figures wearing what appeared to be old-fashioned miners' clothes.

In February 1997 a road spook unnerved a woman driver as she sat in traffic in George Street, Montrose. Her gaze was drawn to a stooped, elderly man shambling along the pavement. The man, wearing a cap and homespun jacket, vanished through a boarded-up window of a vacant shop.

A reporter from *The Courier and Advertiser* spoke to a woman living in a flat above the shop. She said that she occasionally caught the inexplicable aroma of sweet tobacco and perfume. In the early 19th century George Street was widened and an old coaching inn, the Turks Head, which stood on the site of present-day properties, was demolished. Was the ghost a regular pub-goer?

While hunting road phantom reports I heard the curious story of two elderly sisters who as children had seen an eerie sight at the gates of a Highland mansion. One girl saw a band of ragged people, including children, while the other identified a procession of carriages. I was intrigued when told that the manifestation seen by one sister was invisible to the other, and vice-versa.

I traced a sister to Strathpeffer where my description raised a chuckle. Yes, they had seen something strange on the road outside Pitcalzean House in Easter Ross around 1930, but no, there were no ghostly columns.

It emerged the girls had been walking down the drive from the house when they both stopped in their tracks. One sister saw a lady in grey, accompanied by two running children, pass the gates, before vanishing. Her sister had seen only the woman. The figures were heading in the direction of the Nigg ferry.

But what do you make of the bizarre road phantom spotted by a married couple in the Borders? It was a foul night of wind and sleet as they headed towards Jedburgh. Yet in the glimmer of the headlights they saw a man about to cross the road. The strange figure was wearing a three-quarter-length coat, top hat and swung a walking stick. But what made the episode so incongruous was that the mystery man's complete attire, including his walking stick, bore thin black and white hoops! Even as they feared they were about to run down a manic sports fan in his club colours the figure vanished. The driver put his foot down. If it was a flesh and blood jaywalker why didn't his topper take off in the gale?

On his travels the late Seton Gordon, author and wildlife authority, encountered the supernatural, including a frightening night in a haunted bed in Berkeley Castle, Gloucestershire. He also had a brush with a phantom lorry in broad daylight on his beloved Skye.

In an article in *The Scots Magazine* in 1959 he described how he and his wife were driving along the main road between Portree and Sconser, 12 miles to the south, when they saw the vehicle approaching from beyond a bend. As they rounded the bend he was prepared to draw in to let the oncoming lorry past – except there was no motor vehicle in sight.

Gordon claimed the lorry had been reported by many other people both by day and by night. The phantom vehicle was frequently seen at night in the form of a bright light. This alarmed drivers as it approached as though belonging to a vehicle driven in the middle of the road. Gordon told of a mail van driver who encountered the mystery light travelling towards him on a dark winter morning. A collision seemed inevitable, but at the last moment the light seemed to pass right through the van. The author could give no explanation.

In recent years the phantom vehicle of Skye has been identified as a 1934 Austin Seven. In 1987 two men claimed to have encountered the vehicle while hunting foxes, and there was a report of an island policeman who saw it while driving back to Portree after a football match.

A phantom lorry with an 'evil-looking man' at the wheel frightened a woman in the vicinity of Stow, near Edinburgh, in 1956, while a ghostly furniture van was seen trundling along a road in Dumfriesshire.

Spectral coaches have also startled unsuspecting road users. On a dark, damp night in the autumn of 1988 an Aberdeen business acquaintance was driving home to Banchory when, less than three miles west of the old Bridge of Dee, Aberdeen, the headbeams of his car picked out an old-fashioned coach as it descended a steep side road leading to the South Deeside Road. The coach, painted black or burgundy, was drawn by four black horses. It was unlit and there was no sign of a driver or passengers.

The coach did not slacken speed at the road junction but continued across the main, hedge-fringed road and vanished in the direction of the River Dee. Had the motorist witnessed a bygone road accident?

One brave lady kept a lonely vigil on a cold and dark Hogmanay in the hope of catching a glimpse of the ghost coach carrying the warlock laird, Alexander Skene of Skene, who was reputed to have travelled across the frozen Loch of Skene in Aberdeenshire.

Writer and broadcaster Elizabeth Adair showed tremendous courage, for the laird had an evil reputation in the 18th century. He was said to have mastered the black arts. On the sunniest day he cast no shadow, and wherever he went he was accompanied by four 'familiars' in the form of a hooded crow, a hawk, a magpie and a jackdaw. Legend has it that he ordered full gallop across the frozen loch and warned the driver to ignore anything he might see or hear and on no account was he to look behind him. Ice crackled under the coach wheels, while two mysterious black dogs padded close behind. On hearing voices from the coach the driver glanced round to see his master in deep conversation with Satan. But even as the ice shattered the coach reached the shore, although the dogs drowned.

The legendary ride began at midnight on New Year's Eve, so Miss Adair also set out on wheels in the hope of keeping a rendezvous with the ghost coach. She parked her car at the stone bridge spanning the Kinnernie Burn and kept her spirits up with hot coffee and ham sandwiches. But apart from a roe deer and a curious owl she saw nothing else.

During the Second World War a tramcar, bound for the Scatterburn district of Aberdeen, stopped to pick up a solitary passenger, a frail old woman in black. The conductress, Nell Harper, watched her take a seat on the lower deck although the lady's face was hidden by a hat. But when Nell went to take her fare she vanished before her eyes!

As the tramcar was moving at the time Nell reported the incident to the driver, George, who recalled having to stop abruptly to allow the passenger on. Anxious for the passenger's safety, he stopped the tram and he and Nell retraced the route in case the passenger had met with an accident. There was no sign of the mystery woman and Nell later believed she had seen the ghost of George's mother who had died a short time before.

A few weeks later Nell was waiting for George at the tram depot before starting their shift when she learned he had died suddenly that morning.

At 7.15 p.m. on New Year's Day, 1990, Banff schoolboy Christopher Christie hot-footed through the darkness as drizzle swept down Red Well Road at Whitehills. He was hurrying to a rendezvous with his chum at Banff links. The street lights of Whitehills glimmered in the background as Christopher crossed a main road then negotiated the narrow, single-track road skirting Boyndie Bay, overlooking the Moray Firth.

Red Well Road takes its name from the stone, beehive-shaped building which encloses a natural spring, believed to date from the time of the Romans. In the 18th century it was favoured by health-seekers 'taking the waters'.

Christopher, a 16-year-old pupil at Banff Academy, told me he wasn't in the least bit worried, as he had walked the same road many times before at night. But nothing had prepared him for the most terrifying experience of his young life.

As the moon struggled through the brooding clouds a figure appeared in the road ahead. Suddenly, an old woman in black materialised in front of the boy, and walked straight through him! He was gripped by an 'icy chill', before fleeing back towards Whitehills. If he thought he had shaken off the phantom he was wrong. For the apparition reappeared in front of him and passed through his body a second time.

Christopher darted across the main road, leapt the fence at the public park, so taking a short-cut to his home in Wilson Crescent. But the ghost hounded him, and repeatedly passed through his body. 'After a few strides she would reappear a couple of steps from me and go into me,' shuddered Christopher, when I interviewed him in Aberdeen, where he now lives. 'I was very, very scared. I did not imagine it – I am not highly imaginative.'

Only when the youngster reached the pools of light cast by street lamps at the foot of his street did the ghost give up the chase. The description of the phantom is etched in his memory. The woman was under five feet tall. A dark shadow masked her pale, unsmiling face with sagging cheeks. Her hands were clasped in front of her body.

Christopher's mother, Margaret Christie, said her son was petrified when he arrived home. His heart was beating like mad. Christopher never again set foot in Red Well Road, even in daytime. Shortly after his ordeal he was asleep in his room when he awoke struggling for breath. He switched on his bedside lamp and saw a 'dark cloud' drift towards the curtained window, and vanish. Mrs Christie, a midwife, said: 'He came through to my bedroom and said, "Mum, there's something in my room – I could not breathe." He was scared. Whatever my son met that night followed him home!'

Was the old woman who confronted Christopher the wraith of a long-forgotten guardian of the Red Well? Before the Reformation a crone was responsible for caring for the saint's wooden image at St Fumack's Well at Botriphnie, near Keith, although it was recorded that the effigy was washed away by a flood. After the Reformation the Kirk punished country folk who worshipped natural springs. It was believed holy wells were also protected by a spirit embodied in a fish, frog or even a fly.

But Whitehills was famed for a character well versed in the ways of magic. A white witch, Lily Grant, was recruited to help both rich and poor alike. The Earl of Fife was driving in his carriage when the horses became restive and stopped in their tracks. No amount of coaxing or whipping made them budge. Witchcraft was suspected, so Lily was paid to break the spell!

When a farmer believed his cow had been bewitched he too

enlisted Lily's help. She even prophesied the beast would speak its tormentor's name, but it died beforehand. Lily stuck the cow's heart full of pins and then burned it. It was said the farmer turned down Lily's offer to make the offending witch dance on the cow's grave. So perhaps the ghost of Red Well Road is really Lily Grant, the 'wise woman' of Whitehills?

A road phantom, every bit as creepy as the spectral woman of Red Well Road, scared the wits out of travellers on the Isle of Lewis until a murder victim was exhumed from his secret grave. The ghost haunted a stretch of the main Stornoway to Harris highway which crosses Arnish Moor, a wasteland of peat moss and lochs, a few miles south of Stornoway.

There was a strong tradition that in the 18th century a murder was committed at this dreary spot. Two youths attending school in Stornoway went on a bird-nesting expedition. They quarrelled over the spoils, and one killed the other with a blow on the head with a rock. The murderer buried his victim in the peat and fled to Tarbert, Harris, where he joined a ship. Years later his boat docked at Stornoway and he went ashore. He was recognised, convicted and paid the penalty for his crime on Gallows Hill.

The tale was embellished. It was said the man had confessed as he supped at a local hostelry, when he commented on the unusual design of the handles of his knife and fork. He was told, to his mounting horror, they were fashioned from sheep bones dug from a hole in Arnish Moor. He realised the bones had been taken from the spot where he had buried his victim, and that they were not animal remains. The handles of the cutlery oozed blood at his touch. This resurrected an old superstition, 'Ordeal of Blood', put about by King James VI, that, if a murderer touched his victim's corpse, the wound would bleed.

In 1873 a local minister wrote that the stretch of road was avoided after dark because the victim's ghost haunted the scene of the crime, which he described as 'the dread of the whole country'. It was assumed the corpse was buried near a grey rock, Creag a' Bhodiach (Rock of the Old Man), close by a stream.

In the early 1960s a shift worker set off from Stornoway by motor-cycle to his home in Grimshader, a coastal community in the south. It was dusk on an early autumnal day when he turned left at the fork on the Stornoway-Harris highway to join the road to Grimshader, a narrow road with passing places. He had gone no distance at all when he became aware he was not alone. He glanced to his left and, although he was travelling at a speed of 30 miles an hour, a man was keeping abreast of him! No wonder the driver almost lost control of his machine. Somehow he managed to keep his head. The figure shadowed him for the next few miles, only disappearing when the rider negotiated a bridge which crosses a stream. He was so badly shaken by the incident that he stopped travelling to work by road, choosing instead to go by boat.

The man, described to me as 'a hard-headed Scouser', has left Lewis. A friend told me: 'I spoke to him the morning after the incident. I knew something was troubling him. He was reluctant to tell me, but I am a Gael, and he knew I would not laugh at him. There he was, doing between 25 and 30 miles an hour and he said this figure was walking beside him. He was able to make out what the figure was wearing. He said it was a three-quarter-length coat, with woollen stockings to its knees. There was a great sense of sadness about the figure which seemed to be looking at my friend.'

It was after this bizarre episode that two Crossbost men made a grim discovery while cutting peat on Arnish Moor in June 1964.

They found the remains of a man close to where the Stornoway to Harris road parts company with the road to Grimshader. The skeleton, which wore early 18th-century clothes, was of a small man in his 20s. The body was packed in moss and flown to Edinburgh where an examination by a forensic scientist revealed that the man had been killed by a violent blow to the head. The clothes are now in the care of the National Museums of Scotland and include a thigh-length jacket, shirt, woollen stockings and a dark green knitted bonnet. He wore no breeches or shoes, which were either destroyed by the peat acid or stolen. In his possession was a striped cloth bag containing a horn spoon, comb and quill pen, but no money.

As the skeleton was found near the scene of the legendary crime there would appear to be a definite link, even though the age of the victim raised grave doubts. However, it was not unusual in those days for a Highland school to have a youth of up to 20 years old in a class.

But one teasing question remains. Why did a murder, which resulted in a conviction and hanging, become part of island folklore long before the victim's body was discovered?

In the autumn of 1961 I had an encounter with a mysterious white horse while driving back from an assignment at Balmoral Castle with a journalist colleague. The animal suddenly appeared in the headlights of our car on the main road opposite Crathie Church. There was no time for avoiding action as the horse, muzzle gaping and tail flying, galloped straight for us. Happily, no collision took place, but there was no sign of the animal in the driving mirror. Journalists in a car directly behind saw nothing and my inquiries in the district failed to turn up any clues about the whereabouts of a white horse, real or otherwise.

On another occasion I was driving with a photographer to a mountain rescue incident in the Cairngorms when I brought the car to a halt. Out of the Braemar murk appeared a weird apparition. Baleful eyes glowed in the car headlights. We were dumbstruck until the figure moved.

It was a stag, and as large as life.

Drive carefully!

CHAPTER 3

STAGE FRIGHTS

On the road to Portobello, where Edinburgh has one playful foot in the sea, you pass the walls of Piershill Cemetery. Beyond the iron gates your eyes are drawn to a large, upright tombstone of white Carrara marble which stands on a grassy mound dotted with tombstones. It marks the grave of one of the world's greatest illusionists, who, if we believe stage lore, haunts an Edinburgh theatre.

Britain was about to outlaw the 90-hour working week; Mexico was in the throes of a bloody revolution and Ramsay MacDonald was hailed as the new workers' champion, when The Great Lafayette arrived in the Scottish capital in spring 1911. He brought his spectacular show to the Empire Palace Theatre in Nicolson Street for a two-week engagement opening on Monday, 1 May. Munich-born Sigmund Neuburgher, for that was his real name, was 38 years old and at the height of a career which brought fame and fortune. The unknown quick-change artist became a household word as he thrilled world audiences with his repertoire of imaginative and daring acts. He produced objects, animals and people out of thin air. Or so it seemed. At a time when Oriental magic was all the rage, The Great Lafayette delighted audiences with his impersonation of the pig-tailed Chinese magician Ching Ling Foo. But his most popular and daring act was 'The Lion's Bride', an illusion he introduced to the United States, his adoptive homeland, at the start of the 20th century.

The stage was transformed into a magical wonderland – a circus ring or sometimes a harem, alive with swirling colour as jugglers, exotic dancers and fire-eaters went through their paces. The performance also involved an African lion, a horse, a dog and a beautiful maiden. During the spectacular finale the girl, who was dressed in a silk bridal gown, moved gracefully on stage to music from *Lohengrin*, and stepped into the cage.

The audience held its breath as the lion menaced his 'bride'. No doubt blood was chilled as the beast unleashed a terrible roar, and the girl screamed. At the same time as the lion lunged at the girl its skin was flung aside to reveal The Great Lafayette. The switch occurred when the 'bride', in the full glare of a spotlight, crossed the stage and performers blocked the audience's view of the caged lion. The beast was transferred into another cage as the magician entered its vacated lair.

But the bachelor magician was dealt a devastating personal blow five days after he opened in Edinburgh. Beauty, the pet dog on whom he lavished his love and attention, died in her sleep.

The mongrel terrier, a gift from his closest friend, escapologist Harry Houdini, was part of his act and shared his global travels. While touring the United States in her master's private railway coach she had her own compartment. At his London flat, where she had her own bathtub, her likeness adorned the front of the building with the inscription: 'The more I see of men, the more I love my dog.' The mascot on the bonnet of his silver grey motor car, capable of a speed of 60 miles per hour, was a bronze effigy of his beloved pet. His specially designed cheques showed the dog seated beside two bags of gold and the caption: 'My two best friends'. Beauty wore a leather collar decorated with silver strips on which were engraved the name of hotels where they had stopped. The magician and his ailing four-legged friend occupied a suite of rooms in the Caledonian Hotel, in the west end of Edinburgh's Princes Street. After her death, Lafayette gave orders for his dog to be embalmed and enclosed in an elaborate coffin.

A professor of the Royal College of Surgeons carried out the task and city undertakers provided the oak, glass-topped casket lined with zinc. Beauty reclined on a silk cushion with a silk quilt spread over her. Before her burial The Great Lafayette visited the undertakers' private mortuary each day and each evening after his show.

But the day before Beauty's funeral her distressed master faced a far greater calamity. On the night of Tuesday, 9 May 1911, his spellbinding performance brought down the house – literally, and it cost him his life. As the show reached its dramatic climax at around 11 a plume of bright flame burst from an Oriental lamp.

Flames quickly engulfed the scenery and backstage area. The vast second house audience of 2,000 thought it was part of the act until the orchestra in the pit struck up the National Anthem. The crowds headed for the exits as the iron fireproof curtain was lowered. But it jammed two feet above the stage floor and smoke curled into the auditorium. Apart from a minor stampede in the gallery, where several women fainted, the exodus was conducted in an orderly manner.

In the confusion backstage the lion was seen escaping from its cage with its mane on fire. Lafayette had jumped clear of the stage, but was ordered to go back and shoot the crazed beast.

There was no great escape for The Great Lafayette. He and nine others died in the conflagration, which took firemen three hours to contain.

Scots author, the late Alasdair Alpin MacGregor, recalled in his autobiography how as a schoolboy morbid curiosity drew him to the scene the following morning as the fire brigade dampened down the smouldering debris, and recovered charred bodies. The tragedy caused a sensation and newsvendors did a roaring trade.

Rumours swept the city that Lafayette died in an attempt to save the lion and the other animals, but the real events remain a mystery, although it was established that an electrical fault was responsible for the tragedy.

What is also true is that a body, charred beyond recognition was identified as Lafayette by the sword he wore. Because Edinburgh had no crematorium it was sent to Glasgow for cremation. That same evening Lafayette's solicitor, Albert Nisbet, was poking among the debris when he found a corpse under the stage. It appeared to have fallen through a trap-door immediately above. Mr Nisbet was able to identify the body as his famous client by the gold rings on his fingers.

A terrible mix-up had occurred. The man who had been cremated was Lafayette's double, John W. Bell, who was known professionally as C.E. Richards. Funeral arrangements had been made for Sunday, 14 May, so there was a flurry of activity to get the real Lafayette's body cremated in Glasgow and the ashes returned to Edinburgh for interment. Special permission was given by the Sheriff of Edinburgh and the Lothians after he agreed the double's body had been cremated in error.

By a quirk of fate The Great Lafayette had already bought a plot of land for £60 beneath a weeping elm in Piershill Cemetery. He had planned to bury Beauty at this spot, but he was refused permission unless he signed a document agreeing that the white-glazed vault beneath the knoll would also be his last resting place.

Beauty's burial took place the day after the theatre blaze, and on Sunday, 14 May, she was reunited with her master in a macabre ceremony at the end of a sombre but spectacular funeral.

It seemed all Edinburgh turned out to watch the vast procession file through the heart of the city. The hearse, drawn by four black plumed horses, was followed by the magician's own private car carrying the chief mourner, 'Mabel', a Dalmatian dog, which had belonged to the deceased.

At the cemetery Beauty's coffin was opened so that the inscribed casket containing her master's ashes be placed between her paws. The tiny coffin was resealed and reinterred.

But is The Great Lafayette resting in peace?

The old Empire, which was designed by the British theatre architect Frank Matcham in 1892, was closed for three months after the disastrous fire. Only the stage and surrounding area were destroyed. By the early 1960s, the theatre, which had attracted a host of stars, including Sir Harry Lauder, Charles Laughton, Laurel and Hardy and Judy Garland, had become a bingo hall.

On 18 June 1994 thespians once again trod the boards as the reborn 1,900-seat theatre, with glass fronted façade, opened for business. It had a new name – the Edinburgh Festival Theatre.

In the same year came the first hint that The Great Lafayette may have returned to his old haunt. A night cleaner, not given to flights of imagination, got a pretty nasty shock when he saw a 'tall, dark figure' backstage. It appeared near the wardrobe room on the third floor. According to theatre spokeswoman Fiona Duff: 'He was pretty shaken up. Someone from the stage-door came down and made him a strong cup of tea. Everyone decided it was the ghost of Lafayette, and it was taken quite seriously at the time. Although the backstage area has been completely renovated since Lafayette's day, the sighting was made in the same place where the fire happened.'

Stagehand Gordon Brown is one of the night staff who claims to have seen the wraith of the famous illusionist. He described it as a 'black shadow' or 'black figure', which suddenly materialises in the upper circle, and then vanishes in a split second. He claimed a number of his colleagues had also seen 'Lafayette'.

Gordon first glimpsed the ghost in 1995. It appeared as a six feet tall black shadow moving through the seats in the upper circle. 'It could have been a trick of the light, but my experience led me to believe it was something more than imagination.'

Gordon said he and his mates believe 'Lafayette' could be responsible for causing theatre lights to flicker and dim, and the apparent 'cold spots' in the lift at the back of the house.

Does the ghost of Dame Ellen Terry, the outstanding actress of Victorian times, haunt another Edinburgh theatre? If so, she might be the lady in pale blue seen simultaneously by two people during performances of Tony Roper's stage hit, *The Steamie,* at the Royal Lyceum in January 1996. Clare Simpson, the theatre's press and marketing officer, told me the lone figure was spotted in the gallery, closed to the public since 1966. Spotlights are mounted in the fourth-level gallery, which retains row upon row of green velvet seats.

The second half of the play was about to start when an actress in the wings spotted the lady in pale blue standing in the gallery. The figure waved to her before vanishing.

Clare told me there was a woman in the gallery at the time – the follow-spot operator. But she was wearing black and busy preparing for the rest of the show. But she too caught sight of the phantom lady. Explained Clare: 'She saw the figure out of the corner of her eye, and took it to be one of the stage management staff who had come to see her. When she turned to look there was nobody there.' After the strange encounter became knowledge within the theatre company the two witnesses found that their descriptions of the lady in pale blue were identical.

A long-serving member of theatre staff told Clare that she had 'sensed things' and in her early days had avoided certain staircases in the building.

Ellen Terry (1848-1928), whose first stage appearance was at the age of eight before Queen Victoria, performed at the opening of the Royal Lyceum. A chalk statue of the legendary actress stood in the foyer until broken up during the Second World War because of a shortage of chalk.

Some hours after the curtain dropped on an evening performance at the Edinburgh Playhouse the intruder alarm was activated. Police, leading a sniffer dog, swooped on the theatre at the top of Leith Walk to search the red, gold and wood-panelled auditorium, backstage and offices with tooth-comb thoroughness.

At the end of the early morning hunt they assured an assistant manager that there was no one inside except the 'man in the grey coat'. But they were smartly told there was no man in a grey coat in the theatre. It was noted by those present that the police dog was acting uneasily. It seemed the law had met up with 'Albert' the playful ghost.

In 1992 Daphne and John Plowman, of the Scottish Society for Psychical Research, visited the theatre to investigate the reported apparition, as well as 'cold spots' and the feeling of a 'presence', particularly on level six.

Daphne, who was born and bred in Edinburgh's old town, remembered reports of a nightwatchman's ghost in the mid-1950s when she attended college. The man was supposed to have taken his own life, but his name and circumstances of his death were unknown. Theatre staff can throw no light on the mystery, although it is believed 'Albert' was a maintenance man who was killed in a backstage accident. 'He seems to be a cheeky ghost, playing tricks on people,' said Ruth Pepper at the theatre press office.

The land on which the Playhouse was built in 1929 has a sinister history stretching back hundreds of years. The Carmelite monastery of Greenside once stood here (the monks wore white tunics), and in later years citizens flocked to tournaments, revels and open-air plays, such as *The Pleasant Satyre*, performed in 1544 before Mary of Guise.

But Greenside was also the place where the hangman plied his grisly trade. Major Thomas Weir, the notorious Wizard of the West Bow, who was said to be in league with the Devil, was burnt alive at the Gallowlea, where a church now stands at the end of Royal Terrace on the north-western shoulder of Calton Hill. His spinster sister Jean was hanged in the Grassmarket. Their former home in the West Bow gained an evil reputation, and superstitious neighbours made exaggerated claims that the place was haunted by a host of bizarre apparitions and a phantom coach.

A tall gibbet reared above Leith Walk until the sandy knoll on which it stood was carted off to be used for building materials in the New Town. Is it possible the Playhouse ghost is associated with the dark deeds of bygone times?

One of the capital's grandest playhouses, the original Theatre Royal (1768), which stood at the corner of Waterloo Place and the North Bridge for almost a century, was reputed to be haunted.

The manager, and future owner, Mr Jackson, and his family, lived in an apartment above the box office which adjoined the theatre. It was put about that after the playhouse was locked for the night and the last candle snuffed, eerie noises were heard throughout the building. Soon all Edinburgh was agog with rumours of phantom thespians re-enacting performances on a dark, empty stage. It is not known if Mr Jackson plucked up enough courage to eavesdrop.

The ghosts vanished when the old theatre was swept away to make room for the general post office in 1866.

Incidentally, four medallions from Edinburgh's second Theatre Royal (1865) – profiles of Moliere, Shakespeare, Dante and Sir Walter Scott – gaze down on the Festival Theatre's cabaret stage.

Glasgow's Theatre Royal, home of Scottish Opera, has two ghosts – 'Nora', the stage-struck cleaner of Victorian times, and a fireman.

Theatre manager Peter Price related the tragic story of 'Nora'. It seems 'Nora' (second name unknown) had always aspired to become an actress but, coming from a poor family, she could not afford the money to pay for stage training. She did the next best thing and took a cleaning job in an effort to pick up some acting tips from the great actors and actresses of the day.

'She pestered the theatre manager for an audition and, after countless rebuffs, she was given her chance,' said Mr Price. 'She was granted her audition simply to keep her quiet, but the director fell about laughing when he heard her.'

Her dream in tatters, 'Nora' became distressed and depressed by the cruel rejection. To her there was only one way out. She hurled herself to her death from the third circle. On occasions her apparition has been seen standing at the front of the circle. Cleaners refuse to go there alone. The 'Circle Ghost' is blamed for the sound of moaning and door-banging heard in the area.

The fireman died in a tragic accident while tackling a blaze in the theatre, which for a period was the studios of Scottish Television. He haunts the orchestra pit, and has been spotted standing and staring into eternity by the musicians.

In the early 1970s ghosthunter Peter Underwood witnessed

'poltergeist phenomena' when he went to the studios to be interviewed.

A Green Lady is reputed to haunt the upper circle of another famous Glasgow theatre, the Citizens', in Gorbals Street. It seems that about 20 years ago a carpenter was working alone on the stage late at night when he saw the phantom in the upper circle.

'It apparently gave him quite a fright,' said Jennie Gardner, the theatre marketing manager.

Tradition has it that the former 'house mother' or front of house manager, committed suicide by throwing herself from the upper circle. The tragedy is supposed to have happened in the early days of the theatre's history.

The theatre was built in 1878 and underwent two name changes before becoming the Citizens' in 1945. Stanley Baxter, Duncan Macrae, Robbie Coltrane, Sean Bean and Pierce Brosnan are among the big names who have appeared there.

The Eden Court, which takes its name from the Bishop's Palace which formerly occupied the site of the present Inverness theatre, is also haunted by a Green Lady.

The theatre, which stands on the west bank of the River Ness, was opened in 1976 and incorporates a part of Bishop Eden's palace. The green room was formerly the old chapel, where a woman is reputed to have hanged herself.

Soon after the theatre opened a member of staff saw a 'strange, shimmering figure' in a corridor leading to the chapel. He put it down to imagination but his dog, an Afghan, refused to cross the threshold.

Correspondence came to light in 1979 which showed that the former palace garden was at one time haunted by the ghost of a little girl 'to the terror of the people about the place'. But she is not the spook dubbed the Green Lady spotted two or three weeks after the theatre opened its doors for the first time.

Val Falcon, a supervisory usherette, was standing in the first circle with two colleagues when they saw a woman, dressed in green, walk upstairs from the stalls foyer. The woman had her back to them. Val, who was front of house manager when I spoke to her in 1996, asked an usherette to check on the new arrival but the 'vision in green' seemed to vanish into thin air.

Other odd happenings included 'sparkling lights' and cold spots, despite ample heating, and framed pictures falling from a wall and smashing.

Before the theatre is locked up for the night staff carry out a security check. After the last performance one night two female staff caught a glimpse of someone entering the gents' toilets. A check revealed the toilets were empty and there was no way an intruder could have slipped past them.

Val Falcon has heard the click-clack of stiletto heels crossing the brick forecourt within the theatre after the last patron has gone home. She is not the only member of staff to have heard the sound, which would appear to be a fairly regular occurrence.

Val, who joined the Eden Court when it first opened, said of the Green Lady: 'I'm quite convinced she doesn't mean any harm. I don't think she is vindictive, and I don't mind her presence.'

The colourful ghost is unlikely to have been responsible for causing the framed pictures and tapestry slipping from the wall hooks without any good reason for doing so. This would suggest a more vindictive spook.

While making inquiries about the Eden Court hauntings I learned that a member of the cast of the then current show, the Christmas pantomime, *Aladdin,* claimed she was being spooked by strange noises and the apparition of an old woman at her Inverness lodgings.

Perth Theatre's spook, 'The Woman in Grey', appeared in a publicity photograph to herald the stage production of the creepy *The Woman in Black,* based on Susan Hill's novel. But, of course, the ghost was the result of clever double exposure of a veiled model. However, the Grey Lady is reputed to have haunted the place since a fire in 1924, preferring to stick to the older part of the house.

The lure of the stage attracted Colin Logan at an early age. He was still a pupil at Perth Academy when he helped backstage at the town's theatre. By the time he left school he was assistant stage manager.

Stagehands were kept busy, particularly at weekends when scenery was changed on a Saturday night for the next morning's rehearsal.

A favourite target of the theatre ghost was the seating. Explained Colin: 'We would be working away when some seats left in an upright position would be slammed down hard as if someone had suddenly sat down. Then, some time later, it could be up to half an hour, the seats would spring back up again.' Colin also experienced a 'horrible feeling' whenever he used the stairs leading from the ground level to the upper gallery.

But his biggest stage fright took place in Cheltenham's Everyman Theatre in 1967. He and a colleague were working in the sound chamber when they were disturbed by footsteps. As they headed for the darkened stage the footsteps continued. 'We switched on the stage lights and looked up at a catwalk where the noise was coming from. We saw dust being disturbed on the catwalk but there was no one there. I looked at my mate and he looked at me and then we took to our heels.'

One of Scotland's most beautiful theatres, His Majesty's in Aberdeen, has its ghosts. The Grey Lady has been known to flit across the foyer, but her connection with the theatre is unsatisfactory.

'Jake the Ghost' is a more homely sort of spook. His activities are on a par with those of Albert, of Edinburgh Playhouse fame. But there is more substance to 'Jake's' story. Edi Swan, the theatre's former technical director, has first-hand knowledge of the haunting. His Majesty's opened in 1906, but it did not claim a ghost until the Second World War, when a stagehand was tragically killed by a stage hoist during a circus performance in 1942.

In 1955, Mr Swan, a student at Gray's School of Art, which was then located near the theatre, struck up a life-long association with the playhouse. The former schoolteacher told me: 'If anything mysterious occurred we blamed "Jake".'

He gave me an example of what he meant. While working alone at night he would break off painting scenery and place his brush on a sink. When he went to retrieve it the same brush had inexplicably transported to a table several feet away. Mr Swan went on: 'I put it down to weariness – my mind playing tricks on me, but I began to make a point of concentrating harder on what I was doing with the brush, so I know it wasn't happening purely by accident.' Sometimes if his brush vanished Mr Swan would shout: 'Come on, "Jake" – will you leave my brushes alone!' It was a ploy that usually worked.

Mr Swan never saw 'Jake', but some stagehands claimed seeing an apparition on the bridge to the fly floor, and hearing footsteps that had no human origin.

'Lambeth Walk', a long, gloomy passage leading from the balcony to the fire escape stairs at the west side of the theatre, is reputed to be where the ghost walks. The temperature drops sharply here, despite heat from the radiators.

In the early 1980s, while the theatre was undergoing a massive refurbishment, a night watchman nicknamed 'Skipper' had the impossible task in getting his Alsatian guard dog, Savage, to enter 'Lambeth Walk'. On approaching the passage Savage sat back on his haunches with his ears flattened and his hackles bristled. When the watchman reported the problem he was having with the dog he was unaware of the theatre ghost.

But Mr Swan's rapport with 'Jake' had a more serious side. He was alone in the theatre one night during the 1958-59 season when he lost his footing and plunged down stairs. He was in agony and feared his left ankle was broken. He needed urgent medical attention. At that time Aberdeen Royal Infirmary's accident and emergency unit was centred at Woolmanhill, only a short distance from the theatre's rear exit. But Mr Swan knew only too well that the door of the scenery dock was always secured with a padlock and chain. The resident stage manager Bert Ewen was a methodical man and Mr Swan realised there was no way the door would be unlocked. Mr Swan groaned at the second option facing him. The alternative route was by a tortuous flight of steps to the top of the darkened theatre, and then down to the front entrance in Rosemount Viaduct. Even if he had managed to reach the street he was faced with a painful trek to the hospital along two other streets. He decided on the first option. 'When I reached the exit the chain was off and the padlock open,' he said. 'I could not believe my luck.' But when he told Bert Ewen the next day the latter was adamant he had padlocked the door.

Mr Swan treated the theatre ghost as his 'guardian angel' after that, but it was not long before 'Jake' came to his rescue a second time. Once again the scenic artist was working alone backstage when the second accident occurred. He was spraying gold paint on scenery when the nozzle jammed. He tried to unclog the nozzle when it exploded in his face. Temporarily blinded, dazed and in agony, Mr Swan made a desperate effort to reach a sink to wash paint from his stinging eyes. He knew there was a water tap in the property room, and began to crawl towards it. But the safety curtain was up and there was a danger he could have crawled downstage and plunged into the orchestra pit. Somehow he groped his way to the sink. He is convinced 'Jake' helped him again that night.

His Majesty's, which celebrated its 90th birthday in 1996, is owned by Aberdeen City Council. Before being restored to its original Edwardian splendour, many of the strange noises – creaks, groans and bumps – were blamed on the antiquated system of handling scenery by muscle power. With the introduction of new technology the mysterious noises ceased. No doubt 'Jake' still stalks 'Lambeth Walk' and other areas of His Majesty's as he keeps a protective eye on staff, performers and the public. It's a comforting thought.

Before the Byre Theatre in St Andrews, Fife, closed its doors at Christmas 1996 for a massive facelift, Carl Watt, freelance press and marketing officer, told me about its resident ghost.

The friendly spook goes by the name of 'Charlie', in deference to Charles Marford, a former director of the Old Vic, whose name has long been associated with the theatre, which was converted from a local dairy in 1933. During the dark days of the Second World War he kept the theatre running almost single-handed. Like London's famous Windmill Theatre it never closed. As well as managing the place he wrote, directed, produced and acted in plays. He knew every inch of his beloved theatre ('dear darling, grubby old Byre' he wrote of it) and produced and acted in everything from Shakespearean plays to Christmas pantos until his death in 1955. Charlie's 'presence', heralded by a sudden drop in temperature, was felt by actors and stage crew, particularly on stairs leading to the Green Room. Persons who came up against 'Charlie' on the stairs prudently stepped to one side.

CHAPTER 4

UNCORKED SPIRITS

White-walled Busta House, one of the few listed buildings in Shetland, has been a comfortable country house hotel for the past 20 years. Built in 1714 by a prominent island family, the Giffords, it has its own little harbour, extensive grounds and splendid views over Busta Voe, north-west of Lerwick. It also has non-paying guests. For the west wing is haunted by at least two ghosts, one of whom is believed to be the tragic figure of Barbara Pitcairn. Peter and Judith Jones have owned the hotel since 1989, and it was Mrs Jones who told me about its haunted history.

The house once belonged to Sir Basil Hamilton Neven Spence, a former local MP, who was also connected with legendary Windhouse (see Chapter 10). In the grounds of Busta House are stone gargoyles rescued by Sir Basil following bomb damage to the Houses of Parliament during the Blitz.

Judith said: 'Two ladies who worked for Sir Basil as housemaids are still employed in the hotel. They have many recollections of ghostly goings-on, and several other people who have worked in or visited the house have reported feeling nervous and uncomfortable in certain areas.' Although it is rare for people to be frightened by the ghosts, Mrs Jones said some staff have left because they were unable to cope with the atmosphere.

Barbara Pitcairn was a poor but respectable relation of the Gifford family. The daughter of a Lerwick shipmaster, who died before she was born, Barbara was brought up at Busta House under the guidance of Lady Busta, Elizabeth Gifford. On 14 May 1748 a tragedy robbed Busta House of its young heir, John Gifford, and his three brothers. They and two others drowned on a sailing trip leaving the estate of Busta without a male heir. Barbara Pitcairn claimed she had secretly married John Gifford the previous December and produced a copy of her wedding lines. She also claimed she was expecting his child.

The marriage was not acknowledged by the Giffords. However, Lady Busta and her husband eagerly accepted the child, Gideon, as heir to the Busta estate, but his mother was ostracised and died in Lerwick at an early age. It is believed that Barbara's ghost is searching the rooms and corridors of her former home for her son, or her husband, John, or perhaps both.

'On the other hand,' said Mrs Jones, 'many people have reported seeing a little grey-haired lady in a brown dress with a white lace cap on her head. As Barbara was only 36 when she died, and had light brown hair and was reported to be very pretty, it appears there are two ghosts.'

Is the little old lady the guilty wraith of Lady Busta, who is said to have suppressed Barbara's marriage lines? How do you explain the following incidents?

Two guests who have stayed at the hotel several years running always bring their black Labrador dog. But on their last visit they had difficulty with the dog, which was always well behaved and calm natured. From the moment they were shown to the fourposter bedroom, Linga, in the west wing, the animal showed fear. She attempted to flee the room on her own and howled the place down. 'As soon as they were moved to another room she became perfectly relaxed again,' said Mrs Jones. Did the petrified dog see the old lady's ghost?

Another couple who stayed in the Linga room lived in Shetland. The husband worked in the oil industry and they visited the hotel from time to time. Said Mrs Jones: 'His wife, who had always been very sceptical about ghosts, was reading in bed when she became aware of someone in the room. She looked up to see a little lady in a brown dress standing at the foot of the bed. Although the guest spoke to her the figure walked away and disappeared. The guest was quite sober, and wide awake, and was absolutely convinced that she had seen a ghost, despite her previous scepticism.'

The same phantom was also seen by a Japanese lady who was a guest a few years ago. 'She was very quiet and retiring and didn't say much while she was with us,' recalled Mrs Jones, 'but at Christmas that year we had a letter from her telling us that she had a visitation in her room while at Busta, from an old lady in a brown dress and wearing a lace cap. She hadn't liked to mention it while she was here, but thought we ought to know.' According to the guest the ghost appeared three nights in a row.

A businessman, who was a guest at the hotel a number of times, requested not to be put in a certain room again because of strange happenings in the night. 'When pressed to say what it was he reluctantly told us that a woman had come and stood at the foot of his bed several times in the night, and had faded away when he showed alarm at her presence. He was clearly embarrassed and thought he would not be believed, and was frightened too – though most people do not find these visits alarming.'

But a manifestation more extraordinary than the two female ghosts was dubbed 'the awful smell' by Peter and Judith Jones. It occurred when a vicar and his wife and their four children came to stay. The children were shown to their rooms and left to settle in while Mrs Jones took the parents to their room, called Foula, in the west wing. Mrs Jones showed them the bathroom, how to operate the television, and so on, and left.

Mrs Jones was summoned to the room ten minutes later after being told there was an 'awful smell'. 'I was amazed, having just been in there, and went to investigate. Sure enough the smell was really terrible – like sewers and dead animals. I took them to another room, but was pretty worried as the hotel was full, and I would have to give their original room to someone else. But when I got back to the room the smell had gone. But then one of the couple came back to collect a piece of luggage they had forgotten and the smell immediately came back.'

Mrs Jones opened all the windows in the room, and both she and her husband searched the room thoroughly, but could find nothing. The other guests arrived and were shown to the room; again it smelt perfectly fine and the guests had no complaints.

A regular check was kept on the room but the offensive smell had gone. After the guests had vacated the room at the end of their stay Mr Jones lifted the carpet and floorboards but could find nothing that could have caused the stench. But the mystery deepened. That same day the vicar and his wife, on hearing 'the awful smell' had disappeared, asked if they could have their old room back, as it had a better view. But the moment they walked into the room the smell returned!

'We never had such an offensive reaction to a guest before,' said Mrs Jones, 'and I can only assume that there was something about the people or the fact he was a churchman that antagonised some presence in the house.'

I would speculate that the vindictive Lady Busta was behind the awful smell. After all, she had every reason to distrust the clergy. It is a matter of record that her son, John Gifford, was married to Barbara Pitcairn by the Reverend John Fisken, a local minister.

The Foula room was the centre of another mystery. Late one evening a guest rang reception and asked if the guest in the room above (Foula) could be asked to be more quiet. He was being disturbed, he said, by footsteps pacing the floor. The receptionist was surprised as there was no guest occupying Foula, nor was there another room in the vicinity.

The receptionist checked Foula and sure enough the room was empty. When she informed the guest in the room below he beckoned her into his room and, sure enough, they both heard footsteps walking back and forth across the floor of the locked room above. Not wishing to alarm the guest she put him in another room well away from the west wing.

Several times the electric light in Foula has been switched on by an invisible hand while the room was vacant and locked.

An evening receptionist received a nasty shock while serving drink to a customer. As they chatted a woman walked behind her through the bar servery area. The receptionist turned to see who it was as only staff were allowed there. But the strange woman had walked through the wall. The receptionist turned to face an equally shaken customer, who gasped: 'Did you see that? She walked through the wall!' There was relief on the receptionist's face. At least someone else had seen the ghost.

Most of the hauntings and disturbances seem to occur during May, the month in which the Gifford brothers drowned more than two centuries ago.

A chef – Mrs Jones described him as 'a young, cynical Essex lad who always had a sneer of contempt' for the reported hauntings – changed his opinion after he saw a woman 'with a pale staring face' standing in the upper window of the hotel. As he looked at her she faded slowly to nothing. This occurred in the month of May. Around about the same time he showed up for work on a cold blustery afternoon. The kitchen is usually a cold and unwelcoming place at 5 p.m. But as he walked through the kitchen, the metal spoons hanging on a rack began to shake and rattle, and when he touched them they were 'red hot' though everything else in the area was cold.

Other members of staff have reported odd experiences. Household items act up queerly. Electrical goods have a tendency to turn on or off, and the housemaids have reported kettles and lights switching on by themselves. Several times during May the video cassette recorder has turned itself on at the identical time each morning, although it has not been programmed.

The owners live in a flat on the top floor of the west wing. One evening as Mrs Jones worked in her kitchen the family cat, Thomas, suddenly arched his back and started to wail as he stared down the corridor. 'He continued to stare, then gave a loud yowl and fled into our bedroom and under the bed,' said Mrs Jones.

Their son, David, who lives in Sheffield, feels 'an atmosphere' in the house during his trips home. 'He is not frightened by it but says it feels oppressive and unhappy,' claimed his mother. 'One evening he was going down the stairs and past the door to the west wing when he was surprised by a flash of brilliant light from the west wing. He thought someone was using flash photography, but there was no one around. It was evening so there was no sunlight, and all the light bulbs were working properly, so there seemed to be no rational explanation.

An elderly lady is also said to haunt Nivingston House Hotel, nestling at the foot of the Cleish Hills in Kinross since 1725. The ghost story spooked the players of Raith Rovers Football Club on the eve of an important cup tie in 1994.

The Kirkcaldy team were due to play Airdrieonians in the semi-final of the Scottish Coca-Cola Cup final, but during their pre-match stay a lot of talk centred on the hotel ghost. It got to the stage where some of the footballers who shared a twin room pushed their beds together and slept with the lights on all night. It did team morale absolutely no harm. Raith, or should that be 'Wraith Rovers', beat Airdrie and went on to lift the cup against Glasgow Celtic.

Baronial-style Ardoe House Hotel, near Aberdeen, is reputed to be haunted by a White Lady. Her presence has been felt by guests and staff, and entertainer Tommy Steele claimed he saw her while he was a guest during a Scottish pop concert tour in 1958.

The ghost has been identified as Katherine Ogston, the wife of Alexander Milne Ogston, the Laird of Ardoe, whose family bought the Ardoe estate in 1839. A portrait of Katherine dominates the main staircase of the luxury hotel, and in 1990 she startled a taxi driver when she came down the stairs. He thought a woman was sleep-walking until she melted into the morning air. After he had driven his fare to the airport the shocked driver took the rest of the day off.

I was dining in the hotel one evening when talk at a neighbouring table turned to the White Lady. There was mild consternation and amusement when the room lights dimmed and flickered.

Further along the South Deeside Road another country house hotel, Maryculter House, which was part of the manor house of the Knights Templar and their successors, the Knights of St John of Jerusalem, is also said to be haunted by a phantom lady.

Pannanich Wells Hotel, near Ballater, which Queen Victoria fondly wrote about in her journals, has at least two ghosts. In the summer of 1994 an elderly man armed with divining rods arrived on the doorstep and told the owners: 'I believe you want to get rid of your ghosts!'

'No we don't,' protested Mrs Val Norton, 'they're lovely.'

The psychic was allowed to inspect the premises and was able to pin-point 'cold spots' where ghosts might lurk.

When the Nortons took over the hotel in 1987 they detected an 'uneasy' feeling in room number one at the back. Mrs Norton lodged a collection of teddy bears belonging to her and daughter Alisha and the atmosphere lightened. 'It is really a happy room,' she told me. Disembodied breathing was heard in the room and the smell of violet scent detected.

In 1989 Mr Chris Norton met the hotel's most famous guest. He dubbed her 'The Grey Lady'. He said: 'I looked up one day and this strange lady was standing at the top of the stairs.' The ghost was young, slim and dressed in a long dark skirt and grey blouse. Does she haunt room one? A young American couple cut short their stay in the haunted room after they complained of 'a large grey stain' on the bedspread.

This incident led to sensational claims by the tabloid press that men were queuing to book the room – to spend the night with a 'sexy ghost in a saucy maid's outfit'!

Across the Dee in Ballater there is a touch of mystery about the alleged haunting of the Ravenswood Hotel. Before the present owners Cathy and Scott Fyfe took over in 1993 it was rumoured the hotel was haunted by an old lady. The Fyfes remain open-minded on the subject of ghosts although in recent years guests have reported meeting a spectral old man with a white beard on the staircase. At least two lady guests have claimed their hair was stroked by an unseen hand in their bedrooms.

The 'non-paying guest' has been dubbed 'Henry' and 'Henry's room' is a bedroom on the first floor, above the hotel entrance. In 1994 a professional photographer took a series of photos for a new brochure. He was intrigued by one shot which purports to show a 'face' at the window of 'Henry's room'. I have studied the brochure, negative and photographer's viewpoint and suggested the image might be a trick of light.

Then there was the curious incident involving a baby alarm in another bedroom. As the baby slept in its cot the parents, both guests, were downstairs. Urgent adult voices on the alarm sent them scurrying upstairs but their sleeping child was alone. Of course, the baby alarm could have picked up a human conversation.

The painted sign outside the Cross Keys Hotel in Peebles proudly proclaims its famous non-paying guest, Marion Ritchie, in picture and verse:

> Ye came, ye went,
> But I hiv steyed
> Fir three hunder years

An inn has stood on this spot in the Border town since 1693 but the formidable landlady did not come on the scene until a century later.

The former coaching inn has been identified as the Cleikum Inn in Sir Walter Scott's novel, *St Ronan's Well*, published in 1823. The fictional town of St Ronan's is Innerleithen, where the sick sought out a mineral well to be cured of eye and skin complaints and dyspepsia. But the character Meg Dods of the Cleikum is based on Marion Ritchie, who was landlady of the Yett (Gate) Inn, now the Cross Keys Hotel, in the Northgate, until her death in February 1822.

There was another landlady with the same surname (Jenny

Dods) who ran an inn at Howgate on the Peebles road, but Scott pointed out there was no connection with his Meg. In the novel, Meg Dods, also known as Meg Dort, ruled the hostelry with a rod of iron, and would not hesitate to order an unwelcome guest to 'troop aff wi' ye to another public', even if the next inn was miles away.

Scott sang the praises of Meg's excellent cooking (cock-a-leekie and savoury callops were a great favourite of patrons) and attention to cleanliness, and heaven help the chambermaid who allowed standards to slip! Staff at the Cross Keys are still kept on their toes by the ghostly Marion Ritchie, who seems to have a dislike of modern gadgets.

Marion is said to have died in her own bedchamber, now room five. Mysterious sounds and movements have occurred here in the pink floral-decorated room with its low ceiling, and elsewhere in the hostelry.

In 1975, Ninian Reid, journalist and broadcaster, visited the Cross Keys while presenting his weekly programme, *A Walk Through Forth Country*, for Radio Forth. Ninian decided to interview hotelier Alan Jackson in the room. But things did not go as planned.

As Ninian told listeners: 'I was about to say, in fact I had started to say that I don't believe in ghosts . . . but a very funny thing has happened. I've tried to make this recording three times and nothing has come out – nothing on tape whatsoever.'

Ninian, who is now with BBC Scotland, had checked his equipment carefully but there was nothing wrong with the tape-recorder and the high-quality tape. Ninian told me: 'Each time I carried out a full interview the meter recorder was turning. When I played it back there was total silence on two occasions but on one of the occasions there was a faint, high-speed voice. The voice was indistinguishable. It was very odd; very strange and I found it unsettling.'

Had Ninian upset the ghost? 'I keep an open mind.'

Mine host Alan Jackson told Ninian in 1975 of one particularly strange occurrence in room five (formerly numbered three). It happened while a cleaner was working in the room. The door was propped open from the outside by a bucket and while the woman was busy cleaning the bucket moved and the door closed. When the cleaner left the room she had to move the bucket, which had been on the other side of the door, in order to open the door.

A new maid from Durham, who was totally unaware of the alleged haunting, was making a cup of tea shortly after her arrival when she saw the reflection of a woman in the boiler. When she wheeled round there was nobody there. She described the woman to the landlord's wife and she replied: 'Oh, that sounds like Meg Dods.' The girl's description fitted that of Meg's picture in the hotel.

The ghost's reputation spread for Mr Jackson said some guests refused to be put in the haunted room.

In December 1994, two Australian barmaids left their jobs after being frightened by loud noises and the appearance of a ghostly white arm. Local journalist Valerie Walker who interviewed the girls, told me she was convinced they had been genuinely terrified by their experiences. This was backed up by part-time barmaid Julia Coulthard, who told me in 1996: 'I spoke to them afterwards and they were really freaked out.'

Julia had her own story of the hotel ghost. In 1995 the local amateur theatre group popped into the hotel bar during a nocturnal ghost walk. When conversation turned to Marion Ritchie, a glass toppled from a shelf, bounced on the floor, and rolled to a halt, unbroken. The incident was laughed off, but when the group later returned, and the same thing happened a second time, nervous glances were exchanged.

In November 1995, David Hunt, a Lancashire man who was formerly a ski instructor and mountain guide in the Alps, became the new owner of the Cross Keys.

How did he feel about taking over a hotel complete with its own ghost? 'I am sure there is something,' he said. 'I sometimes hear things.' Mr Hunt explained that his own room is directly below

room five. 'I have heard noises which are not in keeping with the
sort of noises you would expect to hear in an old building. I have
heard footsteps and banging sounds as though someone occupied
room five.'

But, I asked, wouldn't you expect to hear such things in a hotel,
whatever its age? 'Yes,' replied Mr Hunt, 'but the hotel was empty
at the time and I was the only other person here.'

A traditional Highland inn haunted by a piper of the '45
Uprising? It sounded a good ghost story. But although the glen
behind the Lochailort Inn, Inverness-shire, is said to echo to
ghostly pipe music, the inn's phantom, despite press reports, has
not been seen or heard on the premises.

A staging inn has stood at the spot, on the road to the isles, since
1650. And the present-day hoteliers have strange tales for
customers in search of chills. Anne, wife of mine host Stewart
Carmichael, described to me how she felt a strange 'presence' in
room six, an upstairs chamber, although the other bedrooms were
snug and warm. 'I felt as if someone was at my back watching my
every move,' she said. 'I am sceptical about ghosts, but it was quite
eerie.'

On another occasion, a guest making his way back to his room
claimed he almost bumped into a ghostly figure of a woman in a
blue gown.

I spoke to a regular who claimed he was alone in the residents'
lounge when the hotel dog, Topper, began behaving oddly,
growling and leaping at an unseen intruder.

These inexplicable events took place before the inn was
devastated by fire in 1994. It has since been rebuilt and the ghost
seems to have literally vanished in a puff of smoke. But the blaze
left an enduring mystery. A bricked-up wall cupboard revealed a
hidden room, adjoining room six, where Mrs Carmichael may
have had a brush with the paranormal.

The last customer had left the Cocket Hat public house in
Aberdeen and the doors leading to the main door and lounge were
secure. Staff stacked clean glasses for opening time next day. A

young waitress, Agnes McInnes, tidied the deserted and dimly lit lounge bar before checking the toilet area. When she returned a strange man stood near one of the pillars. He was wearing a long coat and a hat. At first she couldn't believe her eyes. She went behind the bar but the man still stood in the same place, alone and silent.

Agnes dropped everything and headed for the kitchen to inform pub manager Alex Cormack about the trespasser. Mr Cormack accompanied her back to the lounge but the man had gone. At first, he disbelieved Agnes until she described the mystery man. Her description fitted almost exactly Mr Cormack's former employer, John Walker, who built the Cocket Hat in 1955.

Mr Cormack was thunderstruck. For Mr Walker had been dead for 14 years when he suddenly appeared in his former pub that night in May 1973. Mr Cormack remembered that his old boss always wore a long coat and hat with a brim turned up. He had a regular seat at a table on the same spot where Agnes saw the figure. Mr Cormack was impressed with his barmaid's sincerity. Agnes would have been a child when Mr Walker died so it was unlikely she should have remembered him.

Determined to solve the mystery he searched the toilets and all other possible hiding places, although his dog refused to accompany him on his rounds. He again checked the building after the staff had left, and was satisfied the place was empty.

Mr Cormack told Aberdeen journalist Bill Harris: 'I worked for Mr Walker and he was a tremendous guy. He had a son who was killed in a car crash in Malaya. I think Mr Walker was hoping his son would take over the pub. I remember him saying after his son's death that the Cocket Hat would be nothing more than a monument to him. That's why we kept his name above the front door – for sentimental reasons. It's almost as though he came back to see how things were going.'

Before the old pub was replaced by a new-style Cocket Hat in 1997, a staff member told me that her colleagues still felt a 'presence' in the lounge bar, and after hours one night a barmaid could not believe her eyes when an empty whisky glass was moved across a table by an invisible hand.

A number of other Scottish pubs have resident spooks. One of Aberdeen's oldest pubs, Cameron's Inn, a former coaching inn, is believed to be haunted. A decorator reported an eerie experience while working alone in the lounge bar after hours. The man was painting the ceiling when three sharp knocks on the floor of the room above ruined his concentration.

Another old coaching inn, Hunter's Tryst, at Oxgangs, Edinburgh, is reputed to be haunted by a White Lady. In the 18th century the Six Feet Club, an athletic club whose members had to measure up, literally, to join, met here twice a year for the presentation of silver medals to winners of various sporting events. Many prominent citizens, including Sir Walter Scott, attended.

Eerie noises were reported after hours in the Four Mile Inn at Bucksburn, Aberdeen, in 1994. Two barmen were locking up at night when 'pronounced footsteps' came from an area they had secured moments before. A check revealed nothing untoward but on returning downstairs the phantom footsteps resumed. It was suggested that a former landlord was responsible. When he was alive he loved playing practical jokes on brewery representatives and customers.

A psychic investigation was carried out at The Stables in Kirkintilloch, near Glasgow, after manager Robert O'Brien reported an 'uneasy' presence in the restaurant. His wife, Siobhan, claimed to have encountered the whiff of perfume at the entrance to the kitchens, and it was believed the alleged haunting was caused by a woman. After two psychic investigators were called in things seemed to calm down.

The listed building formerly stabled working horses that pulled barges on the Forth and Clyde Canal. Mr O'Brien, who said he had never been scared by the 'presence', told me there was a tradition that a tinker had been murdered on land now used as the picnic area, but he did not know the authenticity of the story.

A guide to 'uncorked spirits' would not be complete without

mention of ancient castles which are now used as hotels.

Culcreuch at Fintry, Stirlingshire, inhabited since 1320, and the former home of the Galbraiths, is reputed to be haunted by a musical lady ghost who has been heard playing an invisible stringed instrument in the Chinese Bird Room, so called because of its 18th-century hand-painted Chinese wallpaper.

Guests at Comlongon Castle at Clarencefield, near Dumfries, can read all about the resident ghost in hotel literature. Lady Marion Carruthers, daughter of Sir Simon Carruthers of Mouswald, became the centre of unwelcome attention from powerful suitors who were also after her share of her father's estate. Sir James Douglas of Drumlanrig, a man she did not love, obtained consent to marry Marion, as well as her share of her fortune, and tried to force his claim. In 1563 the Privy Council of Scotland ordered Marion into the wardenship of Borthwick Castle until the dispute was settled.

Marion escaped and took refuge in Comlongon, the home of her uncle, Sir William Murray. But, distressed to the point of madness by events, she hurled herself from the lookout tower on 25 September 1570, although it was rumoured she was murdered by the Douglases.

Sir James Douglas obtained half a share of Mouswald lands without marrying Marion, who, because she had committed suicide, a crime in the eyes of the church, was not given a Christian burial.

No grass was said to grow on the spot where Marion was killed, and her sobbing ghost has walked the castle and its grounds. Her wraith is seldom seen nowadays but a 'presence' has been felt by staff and guests.

Simon Ptolomey, who owns the hotel with his brother, Philip, was having a bath in his private apartment when he felt 'something' pass him. One evening he was behind the bar talking to guests when he was suddenly pushed from behind by an unseen force.

I also heard of a painting of the castle which changed colour. It hangs in a private apartment. The sky was pink and mauve but around Christmas 1996 it had inexplicably changed to turquoise. The mystery has still to be solved.

The Scottish Tourist Board in Inverness released a list of Scotland's ghosts in time for Hallowe'en 1997. Castle hotel apparitions include a remorseful housekeeper who for three centuries has haunted a room in Airth Castle Hotel, near Falkirk. She is said to have deserted her charges, two children, who perished in a blaze, and has spent eternity searching for them.

A Green Lady who was thwarted in love haunts the west tower of Fernie Castle Hotel in Fife. She is said to have plunged to her death from the tower, and notifies her presence by tampering with lights and electrical apparatus.

A mist is said to herald the presence of an old housekeeper searching for her favourite chair in the Broadford Hotel on the Isle of Skye. A shadowy figure and the unexplained movement of lamps and ladders have added to the mystery.

At the Gight House Hotel, a former Free Kirk manse, in Methlick, Aberdeenshire, the spectral figure of the Rev. John Mennie, who died in 1886 aged 60, has been seen in the bedrooms and also the bar. The hotel is no distance from Gight Castle, where phantom pipe music can be reputedly heard.

A ghost piper is said to haunt the Colquhonnie Hotel at Strathdon, Aberdeenshire. He is believed to have been a member of the Forbes family who fell from the top of nearby ruined Colquhonnie Castle, which cost the lives of three lairds during its construction.

CHAPTER 5

INTO THE BLUE

Early on the evening of 25 October 1940 the Luftwaffe launched a surprise attack on the Royal Air Force base at Montrose, the oldest military airfield in Scotland. Three Junkers JU88 bombers, their twin Jumo engines screaming, roared in from the south at a height of only 50 feet. The strike force sprayed the Angus airfield with machine-gun bullets and dropped 24 bombs. The casualties were heavy. Five men were killed and 18 wounded. Hurricane crews who were resting after the Battle of Britain were unable to get airborne in time.

The raiders destroyed two hangars and the officers' mess, and with it a confidential file on a famous haunting. The file was inside a safe in the adjutant's office, and when the safe was forced open that night, the documents had been incinerated, along with wads of banknotes which were to have been paid to personnel.

But the oldest ghost story in aviation did not go up in smoke. Despite being the subject of pure speculation and gross invention through the years, it remains one of the most baffling hauntings.

When I visited the old aerodrome on the edge of Montrose Links I heard all about the 'ghost file' from Ian G. McIntosh, of Montrose Aerodrome Museum Society. The society was formed in 1983 mainly to protect Major Burke's sheds – hangars built before the outbreak of the First World War, and reputed to be the oldest structures of their kind in the world.

'The contents of the file were deliberately suppressed for reasons of morale,' claimed Mr McIntosh, who was informed of its existence by his father. William McIntosh, an ex-Royal Flying Corps pilot, was a civilian telephone engineer during the last war, but his work took him to Montrose aerodrome.

The haunting was familiar to airmen in both world wars, and right up until the RAF left in 1957. New staff were officially told in writing that the place was haunted, said Ian McIntosh.

According to aeronautical folklore the Montrose ghost acted as a guardian angel between the wars – always at hand to safeguard the life of a crashed pilot. But in wartime an airman who felt a light tap on his shoulder would be sure not to survive the next flight.

From the evidence I have collected on the Montrose hauntings there would appear to be more than one ghost. In January 1913 No 2 Squadron RFC, the premier heavier-than-air squadron, flew north from Farnborough to begin operations at a new airstrip at Upper Dysart, Montrose. The officers and men were billeted at the old Panmure militia barracks near Montrose harbour.

On 27 May 1913 a BE biplane, piloted by Lieutenant Desmond Arthur, suddenly folded in mid-air above the sands of Lunan Bay, south of Montrose, and crashed into a field. Arthur was thrown from the aircraft and plunged 2,500 feet to his death. It would be another 14 years before the RAF introduced parachutes.

An on-the-spot investigation suggested the Irishman had been the victim of a criminally negligent repair to a wing of his tiny aeroplane. But a court of inquiry into the crash ruled that it was due to pilot error. Soon after, the ghost of a pilot in flying kit was seen in and around the officers' mess at Panmure, but not the airfield. There were reports of the apparition vanishing as it reached the doors of the mess. It was also seen seated in an armchair in the mess. The story spread that the building was haunted by the ghost of Lieutenant Arthur.

In April 1934, *Popular Flying* magazine printed an astonishing letter by Major P.L. Holmes, DSC, late of the Royal Naval Air Service and the RAF. He said that because Arthur's relatives were unhappy about the findings of the first inquiry a second probe was ordered, resulting in the dead pilot being cleared of any blame. Major Holmes added:

> The strange feature connected with this was that from soon after the publication of the finding of the first court until the second court published its findings a strange officer kept appearing to other officers in and about the officers' quarters at Montrose and vanishing completely as he had appeared.
>
> Pre-war and early wartime pilots of the RFC, who had not yet been subject to the mental strain of flying over the lines, were not exactly the sort of people whom one would expect to see things that were not there, yet numbers of these officers saw the ghost, and in some cases it appeared in the night in rooms shared by two officers and was seen by both. One has not met anybody who openly disbelieved in the Montrose ghost at the time of its appearances, and even the War Office tried to hush the matter up. It was generally believed in the flying services at the time that the ghost was, in fact, Desmond Arthur endeavouring to get the finding of the court of inquiry on his accident altered, and it was largely due to the ghost that the original finding was altered by a second court.

When operations were switched to the present aerodrome at Broomfield the hauntings did not fade, so, if the ghost of Lieutenant Arthur was allegedly placated by result of the second inquiry why had he switched his modus operandi? The answer is probably that the aerodrome is haunted by a different ghost.

During the First World War the aerodrome was used for training and the formation of squadrons. Stories of the Montrose ghost persisted, although in 1916 it was rumoured that the airfield was haunted by the blood-stained ghost of a trainee pilot who had been killed on his first solo flight.

The aerodrome was abandoned after the war but in 1936, the

year it was reopened to train air crew, an RAF policeman, Norrie Webster, had a terrifying experience.

He was on duty one dark night when he heard the sound of footsteps ahead of him. His flashlight failed to pick out the intruder, so he gave chase. The footsteps kept ahead of him. The trail led him past the old hangars where he was in time to see hosepipes, draped on a wall, shake.

Webster doubled back in the direction of Waldron Road bridge where the intrepid policeman was given a nasty surprise. The footsteps rapidly approached out of the darkness. He stood his ground and shone his torch. The footsteps halted a few feet from him but there was no one there! He wasted no time in reporting the incident to his sergeant in the guardroom.

The Grampian Mountains lie to the west of the aerodrome and during the Second World War several airmen and their aeroplanes came to grief on the high peaks during night-flying exercises.

I heard of two ghostly appearances which occurred in 1942. A 'NAAFI', a canteen run by the Navy, Army and Air Force Institutes, stood on the western edge of the aerodrome. It was an informal establishment where both air and ground crews would grab a quick cuppa during working hours. It was sometimes the first port of call of pilots after landing so they would rush in wearing their flying suits before returning to their billets.

Airman Alex Kettles was approaching the shack when he and his comrades heard a 'dreadful scream' from within. They rushed indoors and found the NAAFI girl slumped unconscious on the floor behind the counter. On being revived she told an eerie story. Minutes earlier she had been behind the shuttered counter when she heard the friendly roar of an aeroplane landing. It was time to open for business. She poured tea then threw open the shutters. A pilot in full flying gear strode towards her across the floor of the NAAFI. The moment she held out a welcoming cup he vanished into thin air. She fainted.

In the winter of the same year Alexander Hendry, a civilian night fitter, actually spoke to the ghost! On the night in question, flying had been cancelled because of poor visibility, fog and low cloud being the cause. Mr Hendry, described by his son Tom as a 'phlegmatic sort of Scotsman', was employed by the Air Ministry Works Directorate. Alexander Hendry was walking from the workshop at the south end of the aerodrome to the airmen's kitchen. To reach it he had to cross Waldron Road bridge, spanning the Bervie branch railway line, and near the spot where military policeman Norrie Webster encountered unexplained footsteps six years earlier.

Mr Tom Hendry told me: 'As my father started to cross the bridge he could make out a figure in flying clothes walking towards him. As the figure passed, my father made some comment about the weather, but got no reply. When he looked over his shoulder, the figure had completely disappeared.' A quick check of the environs failed to turn up the mysterious airman.

To try and establish the identity of the ghost of Waldron Road bridge one must go back to 1983 when the Montrose Aerodrome Museum Society launched its hangar fund. Three girls claimed they saw an apparition near the pre-Second World War hangar, which, by a strange occurrence, stands on the spot of a First World War hangar.

Ian McIntosh of Montrose Aerodrome Museum Society told me the ghost might be that of Major F.F. Waldron, killed in action in France in 1916, who probably haunts the bridge and adjoining road named after him. Mr McIntosh and his brother Graham, who is the society's secretary, visited the graves of Waldron and Major C.J. Burke, his former commanding officer, who lends his name to the hangars.

Photographs of their graves are displayed in the museum, a wooden building that has survived two world wars and which boasts a fascinating collection of aeronautical memorabilia. The single-storey building was the station headquarters during the Second World War and was subsequently used by the Department of Transport driving examiners. It too has been the focus of paranormal activity. In November 1987 examiner Alistair Hill claimed unexplained footsteps had been heard there for the past ten years. The footsteps were heard usually in late afternoons during November and December.

In 1994 the McIntosh brothers were decorating the building when there was an odd happening. Ian was painting the ceiling of the display room while Graham was on a ladder creosoting the roof when the former heard footsteps approach along the corridor. The sound trailed off in another room and Ian checked. The building was empty and his brother was still up the ladder.

Graham was alone when someone rattled the handle of the front door. He hurried to the door but there was no one in sight. He was puzzled for the noise sounded like the rattle of an old-fashioned knob, while the present door is fitted with a modern handle.

The museum society's chairman, David Butler, and his son Neil were in the building when the latter claimed he saw a shadowy figure flit into an office.

Phantom aircraft have been spotted in the skies above Montrose. One reliable witness claimed he saw a ghostly re-enactment of Desmond Arthur's death 50 years to the day of the crash.

But far more intriguing is the Hawker Hurricane that startled a local woman as she drove on Rossie Brae, near Montrose, in 1987. Because of her husband's keen interest in aviation she recognised the aeroplane as a Hurricane of World War Two vintage. The fighter swooped so low she could see the rivets on the fuselage and wings. She braked, but the mystery plane had vanished into the blue. It struck her she had not heard its Rolls-Royce engine. She reported the sighting to the museum society. A check of RAF records turned up information that two Montrose-based Hurricanes crashed into the bay during hostilities.

At 11 a.m. on Tuesday, 10 October 1995, a Nimrod from RAF Kinloss was diverted from a training flight to search for an aeroplane believed to be in trouble off North-east Scotland. The alarm was raised when two passengers on a scheduled flight from Wick to Aberdeen reported seeing a plane about to ditch 20 miles north-east of the Moray coast. The search and rescue mission also involved a Sea King helicopter from RAF Lossiemouth, the Alness-based target ship, *Seal*, and a small coaster. But after one hour, with no aircraft reported overdue and no trace of wreckage or survivors, the alert was called off and logged as a false alarm. It was believed what the airline passengers had actually seen was a target 'sea sledge' being towed through a military range, Delta 807, 20 miles north-east of Lossiemouth.

The mystery sighting brought back memories of a phantom wartime bomber which has been reported by pilots and passengers on flights over the Moray Firth in recent years. The aircraft has been identified as a twin-engined Handley Page Hampden, many of which operated from Moray Firth and other Highland coastal bases. In March 1943 a Hampden of 415 Squadron, based at Tain, went missing after operations off Norway.

The mystery of the ghost bomber was revealed a week after the false alarm by David Morgan, editor of the *Forres Gazette*. He interviewed a Nimrod crewman who spoke of earlier sightings. David Morgan wrote:

> The most interesting sighting was made some years ago by the pilots of a commercial flight flying back to Wick from Inverness. They reported what they identified as a Hampden bomber flying near them. They relayed the sighting to ground air traffic controllers who monitored radar returns and told the pilots that despite what they were seeing, there was no other aircraft within miles. The mystery bomber then disappeared!

The Hampden, easily recognisable by its narrow, pencil-slim rear fuselage with twin tailfins, was a disappointment operationally, although it did take part in the first bombing raids on Berlin and in the first of the 1,000 bomber raids on Cologne. Several Hampdens crashed in the Moray Firth area before and during the last war.

Mr Morgan, himself a keen flier, told me he was familiar with reports of the ghost bomber, but admitted scepticism. While flying he has seen lots of physical evidence, such as a flock of birds, which could be misinterpreted. 'But,' he added with a note of caution, 'there are a lot of believers out there.'

Mr Morgan, a founder member of Banff Flying Club, told me a chilling story centred on the former club's base, the wartime headquarters of the RAF's Strike Wing at Boyndie.

Mosquito and Beaufort fighters operated from Boyndie and in the winter of 1944–45 a Canadian pilot had an uncanny experience after taking part in a raid on shipping in a Norwegian fjord. It was an attack that cost the life of a close friend.

A few days after the raid he saw the familiar figure of his dead countryman standing at the intersection of two runways. More than 20 years ago the former pilot, who visited Boyndie after retiring from Canadian Pacific Railways, related his ghostly encounter to Mr Morgan.

History was made at Boyndie. The final shipping strike of the war was launched from there on 4 May 1945. The roar of warplanes has long been replaced by birdsong and drone of tractors, but the exploits of Banff Strike Wing will never be forgotten. A roadside memorial honours the brave men whose battleground was the grey, desolate waters of the North Sea.

This hostile environment which has claimed the lives of airmen, mariners and oilmen, harbours one of the strangest ghost stories ever. A haunted oil rig!

In the summer of 1990 Glaswegian Bill McCluskey was employed as a contract worker on Chevron's Ninian Southern production platform, 90 miles north-east of Shetland. For six weeks he was involved in blasting and spraying work.

Mr McCluskey was allotted a two-man cabin in the new living quarters after a previous occupant, a Geordie, had changed rooms. At the time this did not strike Mr McCluskey as out of the ordinary. He slept in a bottom bunk with his feet pointing towards the cabin door. The curtains of his bunk were wide open so he had a clear view of the room. The man in the top bunk slept with his curtains closed so, presumably, he didn't see anything.

Some time during the night Mr McCluskey awoke to find two strangers in the cabin. They were a man and a woman dressed in sailing gear from a bygone era, probably the 1920s or 1930s.

'I wasn't dreaming,' Mr McCluskey told me. 'They were standing almost at the cabin door, which was closed.'

The couple stood close to each other and were talking, although he could not hear a single word. It was as if, he said, he was watching a silent movie. The couple appeared worried and were holding hands.

Mr McCluskey described them as tall, although the man was taller. He had grey hair and was wearing grey flannels, a woollen pullover and white shoes. The woman was dressed in grey-striped jacket, blouse and white shoes. She reminded Mr McCluskey of 'Mrs Simpson', the late Duchess of Windsor. Her greyish hair was brushed back over her ears. They were bareheaded and were not wearing lifejackets. They looked dressed for yachting.

The cabin was in darkness, it had no porthole, and the electric light had been switched off. Yet Mr McCluskey was able to distinguish the apparitions, thanks to a glow shining in their faces. The figures, he added, were solid-looking. 'When I first saw them I thought it was real people who had wandered into the cabin.'

The oilman made no attempt to speak to the couple and as far as he was aware they did not seem to notice him. At one stage Mr McCluskey sat up in bed and lit a cigarette, but extinguished it after two puffs. He watched the mystery couple for fully a minute before they vanished before his eyes.

'These things don't bother me,' added Mr McCluskey. 'After I put out my cigarette I went back to sleep. I didn't tell any of the lads in the morning – they would have just laughed.' After leaving Ninian Southern at the end of his contract Mr McCluskey shared his experience with only one person, his wife, Ellen.

Mr McCluskey believes the ghostly couple perished in a yachting accident. He and Ellen remained tight-lipped about the bizarre episode, until a second strange incident occurred again in the vicinity of the Ninian Field two some years later.

On the night of 26 September 1992, HM Coastguard in Shetland launched an investigation into the broadcasting of a Mayday call, which sounded 'like an electronic voice'. Standby safety ships, which keep a round-the-clock watch on oilfield installations, carried out an intensive, but fruitless hunt. After details of the mystery SOS were made public Mr McCluskey decided to break his silence. He disclosed his ghostly encounter on Ninian Southern, and suggested the SOS could have been a ghostly call from the past.

His strange experience was picked up by Chevron's own in-house publication, *Chevron Times,* which described how Ninian Central platform's radio operator Dave Moxey heard a Mayday call on a distress channel which he described as 'digitised', like an electronic voice heard on telephones from talking computers. Dave told the newspaper: 'The single word "Mayday" was repeated seven or eight times. Shetland Coastguard, the Brent platform and ships in the area heard it too. We put out a message every half an hour asking for the caller to identify themselves but there was no response.'

The *Chevron Times* quoted Shetland author Jim Nicolson, who, on being asked about a possible supernatural connection, said he was 'keeping an open mind' about the source of the call. But he explained that many ships had been lost around the islands and wrecks were known to have been washed in the direction of the Ninian Field, In Victorian times 58 fishermen were drowned when 16 herring boats foundered.

A cry from the past or a stupid hoax? The source of the mystery SOS has never been resolved. A senior coastguard officer in Aberdeen told me that the 'synthesised voice' was believed to have been broadcast by mistake by recording equipment offshore. It was treated as a false alarm, rather than a malicious call.

To this day Mr McCluskey, who lives and works in Nairn, is still unconvinced and believes a voice from the past was responsible.

But something still bothers him. Why did the 'Geordie' who shared the cabin with a mate on Ninian Southern vacate his bunk and go elsewhere? Had he also 'tuned in' to Bill McCluskey's eerie experience on a previous occasion?

Man's conquest of the air, sea and mountains has left a legacy of mysteries, legends and ghost stories.

At midnight on 3 April 1986, Captain Scott's famous polar exploration vessel, Royal Research Ship *Discovery*, returned to the Scottish port where she was built at the beginning of the 20th century. But was there a ghost on board when the wooden three-masted ship arrived to a tumultuous welcome from thousands of ecstatic Dundonians?

Some queer things were reported during the time *Discovery* was moored at Victoria Dock, prior to being permanently berthed at Discovery Point, Dundee, where it is now the feature of an exciting visitor centre. A night watchman and a former ship's manager feared an intruder after hearing unexplained footsteps on deck, but a thorough check revealed no one else was on board.

At Discovery Point a guide told me that some visitors claimed to have felt a certain uneasiness about the officers' wardroom and some even refused to step inside. I can understand some people feeling a little apprehensive if touring below decks on their own. The lifelike effigies of the crewmen are pretty realistic, and might well be the reason why some visitors have greeted the silent figures.

The spiteful spirit of explorer Ernest Shackleton is blamed for the unexplained occurrences. Shackleton sailed with Captain Robert Falcon Scott on the British National Antarctic Expedition in 1901, but tensions surfaced between the two and the final push to the South Pole was abandoned because of lack of food, sickness, exhaustion and weather. Shackleton never forgave Scott for insisting he be invalided home.

But I think the haunting, if that's what it is, might be caused by a far greater tragedy. On 21 December 1901, as the ship received a great send-off in New Zealand, a daring young seaman, Charles Bonner, slipped from his perch above the crow's nest and plunged head first to his death. The wardroom is directly below the spot where he died. His was not the only death on the expedition. Three months later another Royal Navy man was killed in an onshore accident in Antarctica.

In a graveyard at Struan on the island of Skye a cairn of rough-hewn boulders from his beloved Cairngorms marks the burial place of Professor John Norman Collie, a pioneer of Scottish mountaineering, who was thrust into the headlines in November 1925 with his revelation of stark terror on Ben Macdhui, the lair of the Big Grey Man. In his speech at the Cairngorm Club's 37th annual dinner in Aberdeen he did not mention seeing a 'big grey figure'. It was uncanny noises that had terrified him on Scotland's second-highest mountain that day in 1890.

Collie was no publicity seeker. The 66-year-old bachelor's academic and climbing qualifications were impeccable. He was first professor of Organic Chemistry at London University and a fellow of the Royal Society. Mountain peaks were named after him and he helped conquer the last unclimbed mountain in the Britain.

Collie's name will always be associated with the 'Big Grey Man of Ben Macdhui', although at the time of his disclosure he was totally unprepared for the wave of public interest, and the hostile reaction of some of his fellow mountaineers.

Professor Collie was returning from the cairn in the mist when he began to imagine he heard some other thing than the noise of his own footsteps in the snow. For every few steps he took he heard a 'big crunch', as if someone was walking after him, but taking steps three or four times the stride of his own. 'This is all nonsense,' he told himself; but he listened, and heard it again, although he could see nothing in the mist.

As he walked on the eerie 'crunch, crunch' sounded behind him and he was gripped by the most tremendous unknown terror. Fear seized him by the throat, he said, and he took to his heels, staggering blindly among the boulders, not stopping until he was on the outskirts of Rothiemurchus Forest, four or five miles from the mountain.

He told members of the club, of which he was honorary president: 'Whatever you may make out of it I do not know, but there is something very queer about the top of Ben Macdhui, and I will not go back there again by myself, I know.'

He also revealed to dinner guests that a fellow climber, Dr A.M. Kellas, who would later die on an expedition to the Himalayas, claimed he saw a giant figure stride out of the Lairig glen. He estimated the figure to be the same height as the Ben Macdhui cairn – ten feet! Professor Collie also told his audience that when an old man living on the edge of Rothiemurchus Forest heard of Dr Kellas' experience he replied: 'Oh, aye, that would have been the Ferla Mhor he would have been seeing.'

I talked to a man who actually fired a revolver at the 'Ferla Mhor', the Grey Man of Ben Macdhui, the legendary monster of the high tops. The incident took place in October 1943, when Alexander (Sandy) Tewnion, on leave from the army, visited the Cairngorms.

Mr Tewnion, who climbed his first hill at the age of six, was descending Ben Macdhui after reaching the summit. The threat of a storm forced him off the mountain. The atmosphere became dark and oppressive and a biting wind whistled among the boulders strewn along the Coire Etchachan path.

As he hurried down the angled path an odd sound echoed through the swirling mist; a loud footstep, or so it seemed. It was followed by another and another, the three sounds spaced at long intervals. Mr Tewnion was wearing a balaclava helmet, army denims, and climbing boots, and armed with a Webley or Enfield pistol (he couldn't remember which) to shoot for the pot.

As he peered into the tattered curtains of mist a strange shape loomed up, retreated, then charged at him. Without hesitation he whipped out his revolver and loosed three shots. When the 'thing' continued to advance he turned on his heels and bolted.

Mr Tewnion, who was badly wounded in France in 1944, told me whatever he encountered on Scotland's haunted mountain was not connected with the supernatural. 'There was definitely a shape in the mist,' he said, 'but it was just a peculiarity of cloud or thicker mist.' But whatever Mr Tewnion came face to face with on Ben Macdhui that murky October afternoon he is the only person to have 'shot' the Big Grey Man!

Sights and sounds can create strange and bizarre illusions in the mountains, but how do you explain the 'Devil o' Glen Derry'?

In 1941 a highly respected Aberdeen advocate, Dr George Duncan, who was also Hon. Sheriff-Substitute of Aberdeen and Chairman of Aberdeen Education Committee, wrote to *The Scotsman* newspaper about a weird experience which took place after he descended Devil's Point at dusk in September 1914.

His climbing companion was James A. Parker, a future president of the Cairngorm Club. As they were being driven in a dog-cart to Braemar from Derry Lodge, Duncan, who was facing backwards, got the shock of his life when he saw 'a tall figure in a black robe – the conventional figure of the Devil himself – waving his arms towards me'. Duncan added: 'I got such a shock that I felt what I never felt before or since, a cold shiver running down my spine.'

He lost sight of the figure when the cart turned a corner but Parker was aware of Duncan's silence, which he explained at dinner in Braemar. Duncan believed that the waving branches of trees had created the bizarre vision, but, though he returned to the scene many times afterwards, he was unable to solve the mystery.

His story was substantiated by Parker who commented: 'Duncan must have seen something, as he was so scared that he did not speak for half an hour afterwards, and had not the presence of mind to stop the trap so that the driver and I might see the gentleman for ourselves.'

In the spring of 1922 or 1923, Tom Crowley, a former president of a Forres mountaineering club, had a similar terrifying encounter while coming down off Braeriach, the third highest mountain in Britain, and source of the River Dee.

Crowley was heading for the tower bothy in Glen Eineck, going by Braeriach, when he heard footfalls behind him. He looked over his shoulder and saw a huge, grey misty figure. He confronted the approaching figure and, to his horror, he made out the shape of a head with two peaked ears and feet with talons more like fingers than toes. He bolted.

Ghostly music and voices have been heard in the high tops. The late Hugh D. Welsh, a member of the Cairngorm Club for 60 years, and its president from 1938 to 1946, claimed that he and his brother heard 'beautiful music and singing' on their expeditions to the Cairngorms.

In the beginning the brothers were startled by sounds, but their apprehension was calmed by a 'wistful sweetness'. The elements were not the cause, they said.

Scotland's most famous 'open-air' ghost, a bearded sailor, strides the pink pale sands of Sandwood Bay, below Cape Wrath. The apparition, clad in sea boots, sailor's cap and brass-buttoned tunic, has been seen by walkers, fishermen and crofters. The ghost is also reputed to haunt a nearby uninhabited cottage. An Edinburgh woman, on receiving a tiny fragment of wood from the cottage's broken staircase, was allegedly plagued at her home by phantom footsteps, rattling crockery, the whiff of alcohol, as well as the appearance of a bearded figure.

Ian Strachan, climber and photo-journalist, told me of his strange experience during his first visit to Sandwood Bay, with his wife, Joanna, and two English friends, in the 1980s.

When they arrived there were two small parties on the beach, which is only accessible by sea or on foot along a rough track. Eventually Mrs Strachan and friends set off to walk to Kinlochbervie, and the other groups departed, leaving Mr Strachan on his own.

He climbed to a high point on a clifftop to photograph. There was no one in the area, so he walked down the path, pausing only to take pictures. Nearby was the roofless cottage. Apart from the sound of the waves and seabirds all was quiet. The sun was low in the late afternoon and long finger-shadows fell along the beach. He had a tremendous feeling of solitude. 'As I took my last glimpse of this beautiful place and standing perfectly still for some time, the figure of a man in a black or navy hip-length jacket, suddenly appeared.'

The man, who was less than 50 yards away, was short, stocky and robust-looking, although Mr Strachan was unable to see his face.

'It was almost as if he appeared from nowhere,' Mr Strachan went on. 'He walked across the foreground towards the beach and in a matter of minutes he disappeared. I have been in similar situations in remote places before but there was something strange. I felt as if rooted to the spot, not in the least nervous but there was a strong feeling of unreality, not fear, in the scene.' The man made no attempt to acknowledge Mr Strachan's presence.

Mr Strachan, a former schoolteacher, admitted that in 50 years wandering the hills alone, he had never experienced similar feelings.

Dusk was falling at the end of a fine April day as Susannah Stone drove a family friend from Tain to Foulis Castle, five miles south-west of Alness in Easter Ross. At Rosskeen Free Church Mrs Stone saw a shocking sight that made her stop. In a field less than half a mile away a house was ablaze. Flames poured out of the windows and curled up the lintels.

She turned to her woman passenger. 'Let's go down and see if we can help.' But even as they pulled out onto the road the burning house was lost from sight. The women thought their view had been obscured by blackberry bushes and a fence. But when they rounded the bend there was no sign of the blaze.

The incident took place more than 35 years ago but the details are as fresh as ever in Mrs Stone's memory. 'It was a spectacular blaze,' she told me. 'But it was only afterwards I realised there had been no noise and no smoke. I saw no people or firemen and I remembered I had never seen a house there before.'

When she drove into Alness she stopped a man crossing the street and asked: 'Where's the fire?' He looked puzzled and walked on. After dropping her passenger Mrs Stone returned by the same route. She drove to the spot where they had seen the burning house, on a slight rise in front of Carboll Wood. In the darkness there was no sign of glowing embers, or ashes; in fact, nothing at all to suggest there had been a major fire.

Her pet dog, a Rhodesian Ridgeback, and a good animal to have when you are alone in the dark, did not react. By an ironic twist Mrs Stone's vehicle picked up a puncture at the spot and she walked five miles before finding a public telephone. Her husband eventually came to the rescue in his tractor.

The next day Mrs Stone checked with the fire brigade and was told they had dealt with only one call-out the previous night – a haystack fire at Brora. No fire engine had gone anywhere near Alness. Some years later she returned to the spot where she had seen the phantom house, and found stonework beneath the grass and traces of an old driveway in a nearby wood.

Curiously, five years after the incident, she met a couple who also had first-hand experience of the burning house. Their sighting took place on a rainy winter's night as they motored from Tain. 'Just where I stopped they stopped and looked at it,' said Mrs Stone. 'They thought it very odd there was no sound. They had lost a steading in a fire and said there had been a terrible noise.'

The blazing house did not vanish as they drove past, and they were able to make out bow windows.

Mrs Stone believes the phantom house was Georgian in appearance. It was suggested to her that the house was put to the torch during the '45 Uprising. There is a local tradition that Jacobite troops skirmished with Redcoats while hurrying to join Bonnie Prince Charlie's army at Culloden. More trustworthy is the fact that two local mansions once stood in the area, and one might have been destroyed by fire.

In the course of my research it was suggested the local smiddy might have been mistaken for the phantom house. Then, as now, the smiddy is open for business, but, with the days of the farm horse gone, the work involves repairing agricultural implements. But I was assured that even at the height of the horse-shodding era, with the forge glowing red hot, the only sign of trade was a belching chimney.

However, there was a major house fire at Rosskeen about 25 years ago, when flames ravaged the old Church of Scotland manse. The three-storey house, which was built in the 18th century, was greatly altered after it was extensively damaged. The old manse, which retains its original door, did not have bow windows, and the catastrophic blaze was attended by firemen and drew a large crowd.

The present owner of the former manse kindly sent me a photo of the house before the fire. I showed it to Mrs Stone, founder of Highland Fine Cheeses in Tain, who, after studying it, said it was not the building she had seen on fire.

So there you have it. Was the phantom fire really the glow of a blacksmith's forge, a burning manse, or a psychic imprint – a vision of a previous age – suddenly materialising in the present day?

I began this chapter with the famous haunting of Montrose aerodrome, so I will end with a ghost story linked to the early days of flight. In February 1991 the tourist board in Banff and Buchan promoted a caravan park's new tourist attraction: a pipe-smoking phantom!

The aroma of sweet tobacco has wafted around the place even when there were no smokers in the vicinity and one guest saw a ghostly figure near the park's pavilion, which was used by the Royal Flying Corps during the First World War. So perhaps the ghost is an old flier. It may be no coincidence that the land on which the site is located was part of Balthangie estate, near Turriff, and a former laird, Harry Tailyour Lumsden, was killed on a training flight with the RFC.

Ann Burdon, who took over the business with husband John in April 1994, last smelt the phantom smoke during the close season of 1995–96. 'I got up at 3 a.m. to put out the dog when I detected the smell of tobacco. At first I thought there was a fire.' The ghost was also suspected of tampering with the telephone system. Even the phone engineers were stumped!

CHAPTER 6

SPOOKS IN STORE

A haunted supermarket? Now that did sound curious. It might be the last place you would expect to find a spook, but ghosts in the workplace are not uncommon.

When I entered the glittering Safeway supermarket in the ancient cathedral city of Elgin the only thing guaranteed to send shivers down my spine was the chilled food counter. For, in true paranormal tradition, the resident ghost, a caped phantom, only appears in the dead of the night. It would seem night-shift staff experienced strange encounters in recent years.

June Gray, stock management controller, told me of an incident in March 1993 when she was walking down an aisle at 5.30 a.m. As she approached the foyer where a display stand contained a pile of leaflets, they suddenly flew into the air. As Mrs Gray bent to retrieve the leaflets she heard male laughter – she described it as a 'giggle', but when she looked around there was no one else there. She claimed the laughter had been heard on other occasions. 'I firmly believe there is something – it has happened to too many other people.'

A few months after Mrs Gray's uncanny experience admin. controller Gladys McBride saw a strange black figure float towards the door. At first she thought it was a member of staff leaving the store, but she was wrong. Her statement was supported by a colleague who told me: 'It was about six feet tall and appeared to be wearing a black cape.'

June Rose regularly saw a tall shadow flit across the top of an aisle while on night-shift in the grocery department, but her scariest experience occurred when she was working in the delicatessen between 5 and 6 a.m. While standing at the scales she sensed something walking past, almost touching her. She saw out of the corner of her eye a white figure float by. June thought it was her workmate, but a quick check revealed she was not on duty. Although June sensed the figure moved like a woman the Safeway ghost has been dubbed, 'George'. 'Since I saw it I have not been so spooked out,' said June.

Baker Nicola Smith laughed off her 'encounter' with the spectre. She was standing at the filing cabinet in the bakery at 3 a.m. when she sensed there was someone behind her. Whatever it was began 'muttering something in my ear', she said. 'It was a man's voice, but I did not understand the words.' Nicola, suspecting a prankster, whipped round, but she was alone. She admitted the bakery could be a lonely place at night but she wasn't the least bit scared.

Not all the staff believe in the ghost. However, the figure has been seen by a number of people, and from their description Safeway might be haunted by the ghost of a monk or a nun.

The store was built at the east end of historic High Street, no distance from the ruined glory of the cathedral, burned by the 'Wolf of Badenoch' in 1390. At the front door stands an ancient monument, the Little Cross, where law-breakers were punished in the 16th century by the ordeal of the cuckstool, stocks and jougs. The public drew their water supplies from deep wells sited here.

It may be significant that the store stands on land where once stood religious houses occupied by the Grey Friars. The Grey Friars was the name given to members of the Franciscan order because of the colour of their cloaks, worn over a black tunic. Like other religious orders of friars they played an important role in the three centuries before the Reformation. The order also had churches in Aberdeen, Perth and Ayr.

During the Reformation the Grey Friars were hounded out of

Above: Tragic Barbara Pitcairn is one of the ghosts which haunts Busta House, Shetland (*Peter Jones*)

Below: The Cross Keys Hotel, Peebles, an old coaching inn haunted by former landlady Marion Ritchie (*Ninian Reid*)

Above: Mysterious Glen Derry. The bizarre apparition of the Devil
was seen here in August 1914 (*Ian Strachan*)

Below: The Wizard Laird, with Satan's help, crossed the frozen
Loch of Skene, Aberdeenshire, in a carriage (*Norman G. Adams*)

Above: Aftermath of poltergeist activity in a caravan in Aberdeenshire. Note the sauce bottle, suspended unbroken, after piercing the top cupboard shelf (*Jim McAllister*)

Below: The Ninian Southern oil production platform, where a contractor saw sailors from the past (*Chevron UK Limited*)

Left: A night watchman called Albert haunts the Edinburgh Playhouse (*Norman Adams*)

Right: Stage fright: 'Jake the Ghost' haunts His Majesty's Theatre, Aberdeen, pictured in 1952 (*Author's collection*)

Above: Is Spynie Palace, near Elgin, haunted by
the ghost of a lion? (*Norman Adams*)

Below: Rosslyn Chapel, near Edinburgh, where
ghostly monks walk (*Norman Adams*)

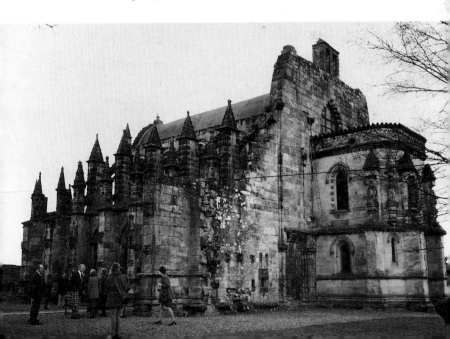

Above: Balgonie Castle, Fife, is the haunt of several phantoms,
including 'Green Jeannie' (*The Younger of Balgonie*)

Below: The lair of the Green Lady: Fetteresso Castle
before major restoration (*Norman G. Adams*)

Above: The haunted Blue Room at Craigievar Castle, Aberdeenshire, is located in the corbelled turret (*right, lower windows*) (*Ian Strachan*)

Below: Ballechin House, Perthshire, was a mecca for Victorian ghosthunters, but did it deserve its ghostly reputation? (*Alasdair Steven*)

Left: Polar exploration ship, *Discovery*, at Discovery Point, Dundee. A seaman plunged to his death on its maiden voyage in 1901 (*Norman Adams*)

Below: Shetland's haunted Windhouse (*Neil M Anderson*)

Elgin by a mob and the monastery burned by Alexander Innes, ironically, the grandson of the founder, Francis Innes, who was described as a 'pious, learned, eloquent and laborious missioner'.

There is no evidence that a monk died at the hands of the Elgin mob but the emotional trauma of seeing a lifetime's work go up in smoke might have anchored a Grey Friar to the site of the former monastery.

Here is some food for thought: apart from the Safeway ghost's cape bearing a close resemblance to the apparel of the Grey Friars, what was that unfamiliar language whispered in Nicola Smith's ear in the bakery? Could it have been Latin?

Before I left Elgin I was told of unusual happenings in another local shop where staff had reported seeing shadowy figures, and where doors opened and shut at will.

A Stonehaven man, Stephen Knowles, saw the ghost of a woman while working late in his family's shop in Market Square, in the heart of the Kincardineshire town. After finishing a six-hour stint as an auxiliary coastguard in 1978, he walked from Garron Point to work his way through orders.

He told me: 'I was in the back shop making up the order forms when it suddenly grew cold.' He rose from the old chest on which he was sitting to make a cup of coffee. 'The electric kettle clicked off, and I thought it had boiled. But it was stone cold so I switched it on again.

'I could feel this thing coming along the left-hand side of the back shop. It was the figure of a woman dressed in a light blue dress down to her ankles, although I could not see her feet, and a round hat with a feather.' Stephen believes she was wearing either Victorian or Edwardian attire. Although a veil half covered her pale and expressionless face, she was a good-looking woman in her 30s, and about five feet ten inches tall.

Mr Knowles' knees were knocking – not with fear but because of the intense cold – as the phantom glided the entire length of the back shop before vanishing through the spice rack and supporting wall.

When he told his family they did not scoff. In fact his grandfather knew of the haunting.

Mr Knowles denied imagination or lack of sleep were responsible. Who was the lady in blue? He dug into the past but was unable to find a satisfactory answer. The grocer's shop was built on the site of stables which served a nearby coaching inn. The area was once honeycombed with narrow passages and the well-dressed woman may have left a psychic imprint while attending a nearby church.

The shop no longer has the name Knowles above the front door nor have there been any more sightings of the ghost. The only spirits are strictly of the corked variety!

'William' was the name given to the spook that stalked an Aberdeen office equipment firm in the late 1970s.

The 18th-century building in Belmont Street has been converted into offices but at the time of the haunting it was occupied by Typewriter Services and Equipment. My own office was at the other end of the street and I got to hear of the strange phenomena reported at number 47.

Office furniture was being rearranged after hours. One morning staff found that a solid six-foot desk had shifted several feet, while steel filing cabinets had been moved clear of the walls. Unexplained footsteps in a deserted showroom; an electric kettle boiling and lights blazing when power in the locked building was switched off and a garage door opening unaided, added to the mystery.

It reached a stage where staff hesitated about working late while some refused point blank to enter the building after nightfall. The managing director, John Williams, a former town councillor, did some research but found nothing sinister in the building's past. In 1792 the original part of the building was the home of Dr James Gordon, a pioneer of obstetrics and a lecturer at Aberdeen University. The house was formerly owned by Provost James Blaikie of Craigiebuckler, a classmate of Lord Byron at Aberdeen Grammar School when it stood in nearby Schoolhill.

The offices had the most sophisticated burglar alarm system in the city, but Mr Williams was more than happy to share his premises with 'William the Ghost', as long as he didn't trigger it off.

On the outskirts of an Ayrshire town is an industrial estate with a factory which security officer Mark Fraser quit hurriedly after 13 terrifying night-shifts. And Mr Fraser, who has been in security work for eight years, claimed he had remained in that particular job longer than anyone else. What spooked Mr Fraser and his fellow security guards?

'I found it a very frightening place,' he told me. 'I would rather have sat in the fields all night.' And this from a Yorkshireman who has done night security work in the London Underground, hospitals and many a rambling old factory. Only once before had he felt uneasy and frightened and that was in his native Hull when he guarded a college reputed to be haunted by a woman-hating ghost.

In Ayrshire he patrolled the complex every hour. There was only one guard on duty at a time. On one patrol he looked through a window and saw a room full of swirling mist. He knew it wasn't smoke and didn't call the fire brigade. Shadowy figures and a 'weasel-type' animal scampering along a darkened corridor heightened his feeling of terror.

At 6 a.m. one Sunday in March 1994, Mr Fraser walked into the factory and headed for the security room, where he was shocked to see a figure standing outside the door. The sighting lasted a split-second but he will never forget the image of the small, bald-headed man in brown robe who stared with 'piercing evil eyes'. Mr Fraser decided to stay in the security room for the rest of the shift. 'I felt safe there,' he said.

It was a phone call to his home that finally persuaded Mr Fraser to leave the security company. As he spoke to his wife Hannah in Kilmarnock, a loud crash and rumbling sound emanated from a corner of their bedroom. A check of a built-in wardrobe revealed nothing out of place, but it frightened the family and Mr Fraser decided to resign that day.

While working at the factory, Mr Fraser never spoke of his experiences to anyone other than his wife. But after he left he contacted some of his former colleagues, who agreed there seemed to be something sinister about the place. There was talk of doors opening and shutting unaided, lights mysteriously switched on and off and a strange football-size phosphorescent glow in the darkness. One guard claimed he was shocked by a dark face with bright eyes staring at him from the darkness of a corridor. But the most bizarre sighting was of 'two ugly and grotesque gargoyle-type creatures' watching every movement of another guard from their vantage point on top of rafters.

Mr Fraser's inquiries led to a piece of startling information. A medium was called in to investigate the alleged haunting and she concluded that the land on which the factory stood had past links with Satanic worship.

Horror or hoax?

'I can only tell you what I experienced, and what I was told by others,' said Mr Fraser. 'When I left I was reluctant to do nights again. But my nervousness left me and I returned to security work with another firm.'

A Scottish newspaper made headlines in November 1994 when a member of staff was spooked by the ghost of an old printer. The Edinburgh *Evening News* headquarters building at North Bridge in the old town stands in an area described by a medium as 'buzzing with psychic energies'.

An editorial staffman was in the basement, where old presses are stored, after finishing work for the day, when the ghost came striding purposefully along a corridor. The printer was wearing matching brown trousers and jersey and a blue apron tied at the back. He was hefting a big, heavy wooden tray, 'filled with bits of metal the size of match boxes'. He was apparently carrying a 'galley', a three-sided tray in which type was assembled and proofed in the days before new technology.

The witness described the scene 'like a silent movie', for the solid-looking printer did not make a sound. The newspaperman fled in terror back to his office, where colleagues were stunned by his disorientated appearance. The printer had apparently walked through a door which had been locked for at least a month. 'He was a ghost – there's no other explanation,' said the employee.

The newspaper enlisted the help of a woman medium who claimed the man had experienced a 'time-warp', a cross over in time dimensions.

Other ghostly encounters have been reported in the 13-storey building. Front counter staff have encountered an entity which brushes past them and have had regular visits from the mischievous ghost of a blonde-haired woman. This phantom appears to walk to the staff entrance to open the door for 'colleagues', only to duck under a counter when anyone approaches. She also approaches from the customer side, waiting to be let into the counter, but vanishes when confronted.

In 1994 a security guard at the *News* had a frightening encounter with the apparition of a colleague who had died four years previously.

BBC Inverness called in the Scottish Society for Psychical Research after ghostly happenings at its studios, a former manse, in the spring of 1996. A 'grey lady' was seen gliding across the private carpark, while on another occasion the apparition crossed the modernised foyer to vanish behind the fax machine.

Investigator Daphne Plowman also came across a case of 'living ghosts'. In certain conditions it has been known for a living person to be reported in two places at once. Two members of staff were seen to be working in the studios late one evening when it was established they were nowhere near the building.

Old mills, as we have already seen, are associated with ghost lore. The Mill of Inver, on the banks of the Fearder Burn, near Balmoral Castle, was haunted by a black-handed fiend, who, according to tradition, was subdued in a bizarre wrestling match with the miller, John Davidson, in 1767. It was believed you could not converse with a phantom till 'the air be let between it and ground'. The upshot was the ghost pointed out the spot where a sword lay buried. The weapon was recovered and displayed in the mill as testimony to the miller's courage.

Upstream, the miller at Quoich, near Braemar, hounded an amorous water kelpie who had fallen in love with a widow. A kelpie usually took the form of a murderous horse which drowned unsuspecting travellers. But the creature at Quoich made love to women while in human shape, until the miller killed him with a 'fairy whorl', a stone security device to prevent fairies from stealing grain.

An eerie tale surrounds the Mill of Weisdale in Shetland. It was believed the building was haunted by the ghost of Lundie, the miller, who was strangled when his scarf caught in the machinery while working on his own. It was said he was found hanging from the spindle wheel which, with every turn, tightened the noose.

According to John Morrison, a former mill worker, whose 1967 taped interview of the alleged haunting is now in the Shetland Archives, the ghost was seen on two or three occasions. But the spook was finally laid to rest after John volunteered to work alone in the mill until 2 a.m. at New Year, without being confronted by the spectral miller.

A school or college, you might think, would be the last place to be haunted, as hundreds of students go about their business. But what happens after dark when the last student and teacher go home?

The governor's room in Robert Gordon's College in Aberdeen is said to be haunted by the ghost of a murdered servant. The room is located in the oldest part of the historic building, formerly Robert Gordon's Hospital. It was completed in 1739 but not handed over to pupils until after the '45 Uprising, during which time it was occupied by the Duke of Cumberland's troops. It was said the victim's bloodstains were only removed when the original floorboards were replaced at the turn of the 19th century. In recent years janitors reported hearing odd noises and unexplained footsteps in the 'Auld Hoose' at night.

Ten years ago strange occurrences at the Reid Kerr College in

Paisley, Renfrewshire, resulted in an investigation by Tricia Robertson, a council member of the Scottish Society for Psychical Research and a founder member of Psychical Research Involving Selected Mediums (PRISM).

The pottery and art department staff had noticed that items were going missing in mysterious circumstances, sometimes from locked cupboards. In some cases the items were returned without anyone's knowledge. Staff and students exchanged suspicious glances but the culprit did not come forward. But the mystery deepened. One evening the head pottery teacher and his assistant were alone in the department. They had stayed behind to finish work on a large pot.

The department consisted of two rooms, a workroom and a pottery. Entry to the department was gained by an internal door at the end of a long corridor, and an external door, both of which led directly into the workroom. The pottery was connected to the workroom by a door and stairs. It was here that the two men worked at the potter's wheel. So that they would not be disturbed, and, perhaps to prevent further problems with missing objects, they locked the doors leading to the workroom, but not the door of the pottery.

Mrs Robertson, who has been investigating spontaneous cases for more than a decade, told me: 'While they were both working at the wheel they heard the corridor door being unlocked, opened and then closed. This was followed by the sound of heavy footsteps on the workroom floor. These footsteps stopped short of the stairs leading into the pottery. The two men looked to see who was there, and, of course, there was no one. This happened three times in all over a period of 15 minutes.'

No footsteps were heard retreating across the floor, and checks showed that the doors were still locked.

A weird happening took place minutes after a teacher dismissed a full class after a session in the pottery. He shut the pottery door and put on his jacket in the workroom. The door began to shake violently followed by a loud thumping. A colleague who had came into the workroom told the teacher: 'You've locked someone in.' But the door was on a catch and could easily have been opened. The teacher, believing the person on the other side of the door was panicking, opened it. Instead of finding a flustered student he was met by a blast of freezing air.

The teachers would later describe the pottery as being 'as cold as a winter's night', although a gas heater was going full blast, and the room temperature had been around 80 degrees during the previous class.

There was an even more extraordinary occurrence. The head potter unlocked the workroom door to find three glaze bins sitting on top of a table. Each bin, which contained glaze liquid, was so heavy it required three men to lift one bin! The potter was the only person to have a key to the workroom.

The phenomena stopped when an old church pew was removed (or perhaps vanished?) from the long corridor.

Mrs Robertson observed: 'The history of the building is fragmented, therefore we could not reach a conclusion as to the cause of the disturbances. I found the witnesses honest people who had nothing to gain by fabricating stories.'

When Glasgow University (1451), the second-oldest university in Scotland, moved from the Old College in High Street to its present site in Kelvingrove in the 19th century, it probably took along a ghost.

Pearce Lodge, which was transported stone by stone across the city to be rebuilt on its present site at Gilmore Hill, is reputed to be haunted by a 'grey lady'.

In February 1989 a university porter saw the figure of an old lady approach the entrance to the lodge. She was wearing a grey coat and a round grey hat. He later described her face as 'shiny-like'.

The porter expected the caller to ring the front doorbell, but she didn't. He strode across to the door and threw it open. There was nobody there. 'Where had she gone?' he asked.

On mentioning the strange incident to a colleague he was told he had seen the Grey Lady .

The owner of the Royale Snooker Club in Glasgow's Rutherglen is convinced the first-floor premises has a snooker-playing ghost! It prefers table number one, I was assured. A woman employee was working alone in the empty club when she heard the clicking of snooker balls. When Sam Crawley returned soon after she told her employer: 'You didn't say there was someone playing.' The table was floodlit but there were no balls on the table.

Queer things have happened since the refurbished club first opened for business in July 1996. Cold spots have been detected; beer pumps and lights have been tampered with and unexplained noises heard.

The club was a snooker hall a few years back and when the former manager popped into the Royale for a game he said: 'I'll have any table but number eight.' The former table eight is now table number one. Asked for an explanation, the man replied: 'The ghost plays that table.'

Mr Crawley, who was sceptical about such things, believes he knows who is behind the mischievious happenings. Before the club was reopened he was standing at the lounge bar, studying plans of the new-look premises, when he looked up and saw the figure of a man in the gantry mirror. The man was between 60 and 70 years old, with grey hair, balding, and a grey beard. He was dressed in a grey suit with a waistcoat, 'like the kind my grandfather wore', added Mr Crawley.

When Mr Crawley swivelled round the figure had vanished. 'It gave me a bit of a start for I had fully expected to see him standing there.'

But the weirdest part of the haunting is that the old man's face has apparently turned up on a security monitor.

During my investigation into ghostly workplaces I was intrigued by newspaper reports of a haunted primary school in the Lothians. On checking I was assured by the headmaster his school was not haunted. It appears they had trouble with hooligans so the janitor solved the problem by rigging up a 'ghost', using a broom and bedsheet!

CHAPTER 7

SHOCK TROOPS

Feuding armies have criss-crossed Scotland since time immemorial. But of all the places where men have fought one name above all stirs the emotions: Culloden. On this bleak and sleet-lashed moor on 16 April 1746 the ragged, weary and half-starved army of Prince Charles Edward Stuart was crushed by a government force led by the Duke of Cumberland, and backed by Royal Navy ships in the Moray Firth.

The last major battle fought on British soil lasted less than an hour, but the Highlanders, numbering barely 5,000, lost between 800 and 1,200 troops on the field, with many more including civilians, slaughtered in the retreat to Inverness. Hanoverian losses numbered 364 of an army of 9,000.

Michael Crawford Newcomen, founder of the White Cockade Society, whose members enthusiastically recreate events of the Jacobite Uprisings, is an official battlefield guide at Culloden. He knows every inch of Drumossie Moor, to give its old name, and has walked across the flat, empty moorland at dusk. He told me: 'I have never felt fear or a sense of foreboding, but you do get a feeling that something dramatic has taken place there.'

On a dry, overcast day on Tuesday, 16 April 1996, several thousand people gathered on the windswept moor, dominated by a memorial cairn, to attend the two hundred and fiftieth anniversary of the battle. For six hours three women friends shared the emotional occasion, as wreaths were laid at various memorials and graves, prayers said and bagpipes sounded a tearful lament.

One of the friends, a housewife, took photographs of the landscape between the Irish Memorial and the position of the Irish Picquets, 'The Wild Geese', whose brave rearguard action cost their little force dearly. When the colour film was developed next day by Boots in Elgin one 'shot' appeared to have the image of a bewigged Highlander in the lower right-hand corner. I have a print of the photograph in front of me as I write. I can make out a 'face', it resembles a human skull, topped by thick hair or a wig, and a Highland bonnet. I can also see the outline of a shoulder and perhaps an extended arm and clenched fist. But whether the eerie 'figure' is a phantom rising from an unmarked grave or a random pattern of plants and moorland vegetation I do not know, but it might have triggered off a series of unusual occurrences in the photographer's home in Lossiemouth.

On two separate occasions paperback books were apparently moved in the kitchen by an unseen hand. One book which was placed in a small pile landed on its upper edge on the floor, with a page creased lengthwise from top to bottom. On another night a different book which had been placed on a low-topped stool had somehow 'jumped' onto the table, while two mugs fell without a sound into the sink. Two persons, the hostess and her friend who had been with her to Culloden, were in the house when the books apparently moved. The kitchen door was closed and they could not hear anything, although when an experiment was carried out in my presence I could clearly hear the book land on the floor, but, to be fair, I was on the alert. Both ladies admitted their sole topic of recent conversations revolved around Culloden and its hauntings. It was no accident that the subject of the books at the centre of the mystery was Scottish ghosts.

But other unexplained incidents took place in the kitchen. The hostess and the third woman who had been at Culloden were in the house after midnight when a 'loud, rasping and clawing noise' interrupted their conversation in the lounge next door. The hostess blamed her cat but it was outside and there is no cat flap. Before the noise began the hostess had placed a ghost book and the 'ghost' photo on the kitchen table. The noise grew in intensity and lasted several minutes, only ending when she exclaimed: 'My God, what is that?'

When cupboard doors in the kitchen began opening and closing at will the hostess sought help from a clairvoyant. On the clairvoyant's advice she hung a crucifix on the kitchen wall.

The clairvoyant travelled to Lossiemouth and made contact with whatever was responsible for the disturbances. She claimed the kitchen was haunted by an old warrior identified as a Highland chief from Skye. It seemed he had been killed while helping Prince Charlie flee the battlefield, but was aggrieved at being ignored by history. After the clairvoyant's visit the house in Lossiemouth returned to normal.

It is possible that the curious incidents were unwittingly brought about. Our thoughts, conscious and unconscious, can cause reactions upon and within our bodies, according to ghosthunter Peter Underwood. It is perhaps no coincidence the woman who took the enigmatic photo had experienced paranormal behaviour in the past. She was brought up in a 'haunted house' in Banffshire, where members of her family had heard phantom footsteps and doors being interfered with in the dead of the night.

Culloden has a paranormal history. In August 1936, an Edinburgh woman visiting the sorrowful spot while on holiday, inspected the graves of the clansmen, where, according to a local tradition, heather will never cover the tell-tale mounds. On lifting a square of Stuart tartan she uncovered the body of a dead Highlander outstretched on top of a mound.

The psychic aftermath of the battle includes the abnormal, but pleasant 'scents of Culloden', resembling roses, sweet peas, incense and smell of burning wood.

Peter Underwood, in his *Guide to Ghosts and Haunted Places*, writes of a Glasgow correspondent who claimed that the ghost of Simon Fraser, Lord Lovat, haunts a small island on Loch Morar, where he hid after Culloden. Lord Fraser was caught and beheaded at Tower Hill, London, on 9 April 1747. It was said his jailer gave him lessons on how to position his neck on the block, specially fashioned for the corpulent Jacobite.

Ghosts of Bonnie Prince Charlie abound. He is reputed to haunt Thunderton House, the former town residence of the Earls of Moray in Elgin, which he occupied before Culloden. His hostess was Lady Arradoul, who, according to her dying wish, was to be shrouded in the bedsheets which the prince had slept in during the short stay under her roof. Past owners of Thunderton House, now a hostelry, claimed bagpipes and voices were heard and on one memorable occasion a standard lamp lifted a foot in the air and moved across a room of its own volition before landing undamaged. Paranormal activity is rare nowadays but present staff believe it is Lady Arradoul, and not Prince Charlie, who haunts the building.

The prince's ghost, however, was said to stalk a Dumfries hotel, now a shop. His army halted in the town on their march to and from Derby and forced the townsfolk to provide them with cash and 1,000 pairs of shoes. The prince and his officers lodged in the best house in the town, the inn which eventually became the County Hotel, an attractive building with balcony overlooking High Street.

In 1936, a woman guest was seated alone in the upper lounge when the figure of a man in Jacobean dress materialised through a disused door and entered the bar. The distraught-looking phantom remained in the room for a short while before returning the way he had come. The tartan-decorated lounge was named after the Young Pretender and the disused door led to his former bedchamber.

The Young Pretender is supposed to haunt Culloden House, which belonged to Duncan Forbes, the fifth Laird of Culloden, who, as a loyal Hanoverian, was not at home when the prince and his troops called on the eve of the battle.

The present house dates back to 1772 but the vaults of the original castle still exist, including a small cell where a group of

Jacobite refugees were hidden before they were dragged out and shot by Redcoats.

The ghost of a man clad in tartan with a plaid of hodden grey haunted the library, bedrooms and corridors.

In an earlier conflict with the Crown, two separate armies converged on a collision course that ended at the Battle of Killiecrankie on 27 July 1689. A small Jacobite force of 2,500 men under their charismatic leader, John Graham of Claverhouse, Viscount Dundee, routed an army twice its size. Their opponents were supporters of William of Orange, whose claim to the British throne had divided Scotland.

For two hours the armies waited to strike. The Jacobites, supporters of James II of England and VII of Scotland, bided their time on the high ground. The wily 'Bonnie Dundee' waited for the evening sun to move round until it blinded General Mackay's troops. He gave the order to charge and a tartan torrent swept down on the enemy. The Highlanders discarded their muskets after several volleys and rushed in to finish the bloody business with cold steel. In the ensuing panic a government soldier, Donald MacBean, escaped pursuit by vaulting across a deep River Garry gorge, known today as 'Soldier's Leap'. It was a Pyrrhic victory. Accurate musket fire by Mackay's troops kept the clans at bay while their comrades escaped, and 200 Highlanders, including Viscount Dundee, were killed.

Dundee's death filled a strange prophecy. On the eve of the battle the commander was disturbed in his tent by a terrifying phantom which, indicating its gore-stained head, warned: 'Remember Brown of Priesthill!' The spectre interrupted again. 'Arise!' it commanded, then, pointing towards Killiecrankie, added with a furrowed brow: 'I'll meet thee yonder!'

Who was 'Brown of Priesthill?' John Brown died for his religious beliefs in 1685, murdered, it was said, by Viscount Dundee's own hand when a firing squad refused to shoot the Covenanter in cold blood.

In Edinburgh Castle, Dundee's ghost startled an old friend, the

Earl of Balcarres, at the precise moment the commander was killed at Killiecrankie.

The craggy, steep slopes and tumbling River Garry weave a spell over visitors to the battle scene at the Pass of Killiecrankie, part of which, like Culloden Moor, is in the care of the National Trust for Scotland. An Aberdeen couple who strayed from the scene of the battle described to me how they were overcome by a sense of menace and did not tarry.

After-images of conflicts stretching back to the days of the Romans, Picts and Vikings might have been witnessed in many parts of Scotland. The tramp of marching feet and the blast of trumpets are said to have been heard close to old Roman roads.

I investigated a report that a party of primary schoolchildren from Hamilton had a paranormal experience while visiting the Roman ruins in Strathclyde Country Park in Motherwell. After their visit some pupils wrote essays describing a Roman chariot they had seen cross a bridge. The teacher checked with the park ranger and was told similar reports had been received from other witnesses. When the alleged sightings were made public the park received visits from ghosthunters. Alas, the whole story was pure fiction, dreamt up by an enterprising journalist for an April Fool's Day story. 'I would have liked it to have been true', sighed a park ranger.

In 1991 a ghostly Viking warrior startled an Aberdeenshire housewife near Maud, a region frequently plundered by Norsemen between the ninth and 12th centuries. The woman was preparing to go to bed when she saw through the window the solid figure of the Viking walking across the yard and disappear through the wall of a steading. He had long blond hair and a beard and carried a round shield. His helmet resembled 'an upturned egg', for, contrary to popular belief, Vikings did not favour horned headwear. A few weeks later the woman was exercising her dogs at night when the figure made another appearance. 'The figure was not malevolent,' she told me. 'He marched in a business-like manner, and didn't make a sound before vanishing.'

Dunnichen Hill, and the fields around it, which make up the

site of the Dark Age battle of Nechtansmere, east of Forfar in Angus, is haunted, if we believe a classic case of time-dislocation experienced by a middle-aged spinster on 2 January 1950.

Miss E.F. Smith was forced to abandon her car eight miles from her home in Letham after it skidded into a ditch. Her sole companion on the lonely trek past snow-covered fields and silent farmhouses was her pet poodle, which she was forced to carry. Half a mile from Letham village she saw distant lights on Dunnichen Hill, where in AD 685 a Pictish army destroyed the Northumbrians. As she drew closer she clearly saw ancient warriors carrying flaming torches as they searched the corpse-strewn battlefield for their own dead.

Twenty-one years after her eerie experience Dr James McHarg, an eminent psychiatrist, interviewed Miss Smith, who has since died, for *The Journal of the Society for Psychical Research.* Writing in the *Scots Magazine* in 1980, Dr McHarg believed Miss Smith's experience was genuine and that she had been in an altered state of consciousness at the time.

But consider the terrifying apparition which emerged from a Banffshire hillside where more than four centuries ago a little remembered battle was fought between rebel nobles and supporters of King James VI.

The burn of Alltacoileachan lends its name to the battle which was fought on 3 October 1594. Historians also refer to the conflict between George Gordon, sixth Earl of Huntly, and George Hay, Earl of Erroll, on one side and the royalists under the inexperienced Earl of Argyll on the other, as the Battle of Glenlivet. The outcome was a triumph of sorts for Huntly, but the king took swift revenge and hounded his opponents from the country after demolishing their castles.

One night in November 1900 a young servant lass and a companion took the drove road to Tomnavoulin which meant they had to cross the battlefield. As the couple walked over the ground the body of a man dressed in white rolled down the brae before them. It was headless.

The horrified girl pointed at the body and cried: 'Dae ye see that? Dinna ye see't noo? Surely ye canna but see't?' To add to her fear the headless ghost got to its feet and ran towards the stream, where it vanished. Her companion was totally unaware of the ghost.

Before we write off the incident as a prank or tall story we might consider that during the gory encounter Huntly's uncle, Sir Patrick Gordon of Auchindoun, had his head cut off in the heat of battle, and Huntly's standard-bearer was cut in half.

One of the most important battles fought on Scottish soil took place at Langside on 13 May 1568 when the army of Mary, Queen of Scots, was routed by a smaller force led by her half-brother, the Regent Moray.

Eleven days earlier Mary had made a daring escape from her castle prison on Loch Leven, only to watch her troops cut down at Langside, a defeat that condemned her to exile and execution in England. The scene of the conflict, which lies in Queen's Park, off Pollokshaws Road, Glasgow, is said to be haunted on the anniversary of the battle by a horde of phantom soldiers.

Judith Bowers, who conducts ghost and murder walking tours around Glasgow, visited the site with friends on the anniversary of the battle in 1993. A tall granite monument commemorates the battle, which was fought over marshy terrain, and part of the site is covered by a boating pond in the public park.

On the stroke of midnight, Judith, who is psychic, and her friends saw a white mist emerge from the pond, and she claimed they could distinguish the faint outline of the heads of the warring troops. After about 20 minutes the phenomenon faded. She has spoken to a number of local people and some have claimed they had witnessed apparitions emerge from the pond. There is a tradition that when the Victorian park first opened the wife of the head keeper saw the ragged and mutilated troops, some minus heads and arms, march across the park!

Visions and sounds of phantom armies, believed to be harbingers of the bloody Scottish Civil Wars, were recorded by credible witnesses in North-east Scotland more than three centuries ago.

The strange events in the winter of 1637–38 were faithfully noted by a country parson, James Gordon of Rothiemay, historian and compiler of some of the earliest maps of Scottish towns. Pastor Gordon was given a first-hand account of the ghostly host of cavalry and infantry which emerged from the mist at Brimmond Hill, near Aberdeen, on the morning of 12 February 1643. His informant, William Anderson, a tenant farmer at Craibstone, said a 'gryte' army appeared at eight and remained visible until sunrise when it melted into the moss. On the same day a similar vision was seen in the sky above the moss at Forfar.

The strange manifestations spread through the north-east, with the 'tonking' of drums heard at Drum and Ellon, where the local minister's supper was interrupted by the phenomenon.

At the Barmekin, a hill fort overlooking Echt, the erudite minister said that 'the parade and retiring of guards, their tattoos, their reveilles and marches, were all distinctly heard'.

The first shots between the Covenanters and Royalists produced further visions. Phantom armies clashed one night on the hill of Maunderlea, near Banff. The sights and sounds of the conflict were so realistic that country folk buried their valuables.

But phantom warriors of the Scottish Civil Wars have not entirely faded from the scene. In recent years I heard that a family arrived home after a night at the theatre to interrupt a strange encounter.

In the middle of the lounge in their modern home in a Renfrewshire town, the apparitions of a Roundhead and a Royalist were locked in a life-and-death duel. The duellists vanished at the flick of a light switch. A psychic investigator approached the family but was unable to glean any further information.

On a bright summer's day in 1932 George Millar and his brother were playing on Aberdeen Links when a vast ghost army manifested on the ridge of the Broad Hill, a prominent landmark which offers a spectacular view of the North Sea and land as far as the eye can see. The boys had stretched out on the grassy links after frolicking with their grandmother's pet collie dog. But when they looked across to the hill they were delighted to see a great gathering of soldiers shouldering arms. The sun gleamed on their bayonets and on the bandoliers of some mounted troops.

The excited brothers scrambled to the summit but there was no trace of the soldiers. An old man shook his head with disbelief and told them no soldiers had been on the hill and he had been there all forenoon. Mr Millar, writing more than half a century later, said he and his brother had searched the entire hill, but the army they had seen from the links had simply vanished.

The brothers could have experienced a collective hallucination. But Mr Millar came across another possible solution while serving as a naval radar rating during the Second World War. During his watch the radar picked up signals indicating land just ahead of his ship, although Bombay, its destination, was still five days' sailing away. Because of a trick of nature the signal had created an illusory image. Mr Millar discussed his boyhood 'vision' with the chief radar mechanic who suggested that what he had seen on the Broad Hill had actually taken place, although hundreds of miles from Aberdeen, and, by a quirk of light had somehow been projected onto the hill.

Military life has its fair share of haunted barracks. In Aberdeen, the old militia barracks in King Street, now the headquarters of Grampian Transport, is haunted by the ghost of Captain Beaton, who is said to have hanged himself in the south tower during the First World War.

In the 1970s bus drivers avoided eating alone in the staff canteen while cleaners shunned a certain part of the building. Staff caught glimpses of a Highland soldier.

After hostilities the building was handed back to Aberdeen town council and, because of a housing shortage, part of the barracks provided homes for civilians.

The story of the tragic death of Captain Beaton was well known in the 1920s. Aberdeen-born May Cooper lived in the former officers' quarters as a child and recalled how she dreaded going to the loft when washing was dried in bad weather. 'I was terrified to go up there because it was said there was a ghost,' said Mrs Cooper. 'It was inclined to be dark and the washing made it very spooky.'

One Aberdeen lady, Helen Leiper, had first-hand experience of the ghost. She saw the apparition, and she remembered the incident clearly when I spoke to her. 'We were visiting my mother's aunt who lived in the barracks. I got bored with grown-up gossip and wandered upstairs on my own.'

Young Helen stopped at an open doorway and looked inside a small room. Daylight streamed into the room in which there stood an iron cot with a white cover. Sitting on the bed was a soldier. 'He was wearing a khaki uniform, he was not in the kilt,' said Mrs Leiper. 'He had a bandage round his head and he appeared to be winding another bandage around his hands. I never saw his feet.' He rose without a word and vanished into thin air.

Helen ran downstairs to tell the adults, but they did not believe her. It was not until many years later that she read that others had seen the ghost.

In January 1915 officers and men of the Highland Artillery Brigade were 'spooked' by a ghost rapping on the ground-floor windows of their billet, a large house called Belfield, near Perth. On a bright frosty night they caught a glimpse of the bizarre figure 'flitting' across the lawn which was deep in snow. The sentries were unable to catch the intruder who left no tell-tale footprints.

Paranoia crept in, and some young officers sat up one or two nights afterwards nursing loaded revolvers. The commanding officer received several requests for transfers. Shortly afterwards the CO was in a Perth club when a lawyer approached him and asked: 'I understand the Belfield ghost has appeared again?' He then told the officer that the house had been difficult to let for many years on account of the knocking at the windows.

There is an echo of the Belfield haunting in the 'spooking' of a detachment of troops garrisoned at Delgatie Castle, near Turriff, during the Second World War. The castle has been the seat of the

Clan Hay for seven centuries. The Hays of Erroll had a fearsome reputation in war, and their very name is Gaelic for 'wall', given to three heroic clan members who stood firm against invading Danes at the Battle of Luncarty.

The laird, Captain John Hay of Delgatie, told me that on two dreich nights the troops hastily collected their weapons and fled outdoors. As the soldiers, some in bare feet, waited in the dripping darkness a search was made of the five-storey tower house, reputed to be haunted by a female ghost.

In 1957 the tenants of a Montrose council house were shocked when a red-coated soldier of the Napoleonic Wars walked through the walls of their home, which stood on the site of the old militia barracks. Church of Scotland minister, the Rev. Frederick Kennedy, of the local Old Parish Church, was asked to help. He conducted a 'bell, book and candle' service in an effort to rid the house of its ghost, but I do not know the outcome.

The coastal fortress of Fort George, near Inverness, is a grim reminder of the government's plan to subdue the Highlands after the '45 Uprising. The fort has been in military use since it was completed in 1769. Legend has it that the architect, under orders that no part of the building should be seen from the sea, shot himself after he rowed out into the Moray Firth and spotted a chimney!

'The Fort', as every old soldier and young recruit knows, is supposed to be haunted by a phantom piper.

But Fort George features a strange but true story concerning a human skull which seems to possess uncanny powers. The skull is on display in the regimental museum. From 1881 to 1961 the fort was the depot of the Seaforth Highlanders, who amalgamated with the Cameron Highlanders to become the Queen's Own Highlanders. In 1994 the regiments merged with the Gordon Highlanders to form The Highlanders (Seaforths, Gordons and Camerons).

More than 30 years ago a young Queen's Own Highlander officer, now General Sir Jeremy Mackenzie, KCB, OBE, Deputy

Supreme Allied Commander Europe, served in Borneo with the Iban Border Scouts, as part of an SAS operation. His task was to train local tribesmen from the Murut tribe to act as scouts in a remote and uninhabited part of Brunei during trouble between Britain and Indonesia. He lived with the primitive Murut natives in their longhouses and at the end of his tour of duty the local Murut chief presented him with the skull, one of many which hung in wicker baskets on poles supporting the roof of a longhouse.

Complete skulls belonged to revered ancestors. But the skull gifted to him had its lower jaw missing. This particular skull was that of a Chinese killed by a blowpipe dart during the rebellious times of Sir James Brooke (1803–68), empire builder and first English Rajah of Sarawak.

The skull was brought back by Sir Jeremy who left it with his mother in Dorset. Sir Jeremy, writing to me in 1996, said:

> My mother was less than delighted with this artifact, and was unimpressed when I explained that the tradition of the longhouses from where these skulls originated was that once every six months or so they would all be taken down and walked round the longhouse with due ceremony. This allowed the spirit attached to the skull to see any new additions to the building, and thereby not become restless. They also took the opportunity to smoke them and thus preserve the bone. They firmly believed that if this process was not followed through the spirits would break up the longhouse. The chief for his part believed that by giving me the skull he did me a great honour in that he gave me the spirit that came with the skull, in perpetuity.

But Sir Jeremy's mother, apparently unimpressed by this explanation, relegated the skull to the attic. Over the next few days considerable damage occurred in their home. Pictures fell from walls and a glass decanter which had been in the family for several generations shattered into two pieces. Sir Jeremy added:

At this my mother decided that enough was enough, and I was instructed to send the skull to Fort George with clear instructions that it should be taken round the museum before being stashed in a cabinet, otherwise I would not be responsible for the damage that might occur!

But his grim warning seems to have been lost with the passage of time.

Colonel Angus Fairrie, curator of the museum at Fort George, told me the skull languished in its box until around 1978 when it was decided to put the object on display along with other souvenirs of the Borneo campaign. But a series of unfortunate mishaps to museum personnel and property occurred and the skull was put back in the box.

In time Colonel Fairrie visited Stanley Barracks in Hong Kong where he mentioned the setbacks to the donor of the macabre exhibit, who explained the object was regarded as 'tremendously benign' but it liked to know where it was.

So, on a bleak winter's evening on his return to Scotland, Colonel Fairrie set about making the skull feel right at home. With the grisly object under his arm he walked around the museum building. There were not many people around to witness the macabre ritual but he swore he saw the curtains of the regimental sergeant-major's office twitch!

'It's a curious thing,' remarked Colonel Fairrie, 'but afterwards everything went swimmingly well.'

When I suggested I might take a photograph of the skull he replied: 'I should keep well clear!' I heeded his advice.

I leave the last word on the story of the 'Restless Skull of Fort George' to Sir Jeremy, who said the skull's 'physical properties belong to the museum, but I am sure that my Borneo headman firmly believes that one day I will be in need of a Chinese orderly in the next world, and he has made the necessary arrangements for this'!

CHAPTER 8

HOLY TERRORS

On the rim of the steeply tree-clad Esk Valley, Rosslyn Chapel, south of Edinburgh, is an enchanted place of myth, legend and mystery. It was founded by Earl William St Clair, Prince of Orkney, in 1446, whose grandfather, Prince Henry Sinclair, is reputed to have discovered America in 1398, almost a century before Christopher Columbus. Another member of the illustrious family, Sir William de St Clair, was killed by Moors in Spain in 1330 while conveying the heart of Robert the Bruce to the Holy Land.

The chapel's delicately wrought carvings have drawn pilgrims to Rosslyn for centuries. The exquisite Apprentice Pillar is named after an apprentice mason who was murdered by his jealous master. According to the legend, the master mason had been commanded by his patron to copy from a model the beautifully carved pillar in a foreign church. The mason insisted on seeing the original and when he returned to Rosslyn he found that his apprentice had completed the Apprentice Pillar, which had come to him in a dream.

In a fit of fury the master struck the apprentice dead with his mallet, and he hanged for his crime. There may be a grain of truth in the fascinating story for the Bishop of St Andrews obtained the Pope's permission to delay the consecration of the chapel because a violent deed had taken place there, although the details have not been handed down.

The carved heads of the three players in the drama, the apprentice, complete with cruel head wound, his mother and the murderer can be picked out by visitors to the chapel, which is adorned with symbolism of Freemasonry and the Knights Templar, a religious military order founded in the twelfth century to protect Christian pilgrims to the Holy Land. Carvings of exotic plants from the New World predate the transatlantic voyage of Columbus.

Wedding guests were gathering when I visited the chapel. It was a place of joy, bright flowers and candlelight. But it was a cold winter's morning when Judith Fisken, archivist and secretary of the Friends of Rosslyn, entered the chapel and saw the ghost of a monk. Judith, who was curator until 1996, was checking the building first thing. After unlocking the north door she switched on the electric lighting which illuminates the intricate carvings.

As she entered the chapel she looked to her right and saw the figure of a man standing at the entrance to the baptistry. She believed it to be the Reverend Edward Downing, the Episcopal priest in charge, who, apart from Judith, was the only other key holder. Only the figure was wearing a black cape and headgear favoured by priests in a bygone age.

She wished the man good morning and resumed switching on lights. The man made no reply. Moments later she entered the baptistry to make a cup of coffee for the priest but the room was empty. 'The figure was as solid as you or I,' Mrs Fisken said. The baptistry door was locked and Mrs Fisken is convinced there was no way he could have slipped past her to exit by the north door. Edward Downing, now deceased, was also the sort of person who would have acknowledged her. He rarely visited the chapel before Mrs Fisken opened it for visitors. She spoke to the priest later that day and he confirmed he had been nowhere near the place. 'He just laughed when I told him.'

Mrs Fisken believes the mysterious figure was wearing the apparel of the Order of Augustine monks, the Black Canons. Six months later Mrs Fisken saw a second ghost monk. He was dressed in a grey habit with a hood, and she thought he probably belonged to the Order of Benedictines or Cistercians (of course, he might have been a Grey Friar).

It was on a hot summer's day and the doors of the chapel were thrown open to allow air to circulate throughout the stuffy interior. There was a number of visitors mingling as Mrs Fisken and a middle-aged woman chatted at the choir in the middle of the chapel. Said Mrs Fisken: 'We were looking in the direction of the altar when a monk in grey and wearing a hood appeared at the back of the altar.' The monk walked in the direction of the Lady Chapel, also known as the retro-choir.

The woman visitor asked: 'Do you get many monks here?' Mrs Fisken told her monks did visit. 'He looks a bit lost,' she added and, leaving the visitor, went off to see if the monk required help. She lost sight of the monk behind a pillar but when she searched the Lady's Chapel there was no sign of him. 'He looked solid enough,' said Mrs Fisken, 'but I did not see his face because it was hidden by the hood. I questioned my staff but nobody else had seen the monk.'

Her experiences took place in the late 1980s. The grey monk has been seen both inside and outside the chapel on other occasions. An identical figure was spotted crossing Gardeners Brae, and during an evening service in the early 1990s a member of the congregation saw the ghost standing in the south doorway. The door was locked and a curtain draped across the threshold.

One March morning in 1982 Mrs Fisken, who had been newly appointed curator, was busy cleaning and tidying the interior of the chapel. A new tourist season was only a few days away. Her husband, Andrew, was outside sweeping up wind-blown leaves. He was working in the north-west corner of the grounds, when, out of the corner of his right eye, he saw a figure in a dark brown shawl or hood, the sort worn by monks. The person was stooped like a hunchback and shambled with his head thrust forward. The strange figure disappeared from view, heading it seemed for the south-west corner of the chapel.

Mr Fisken was taken aback moments later when his wife stormed out of the north door and accused him of trying to scare her by knocking on the south door. 'It was a terrible banging,' Mrs Fisken told me. 'The door was sealed, and never opened, and I thought Andrew was playing a practical joke by trying to give me the creeps.'

No sign of the stranger was ever found. Mr Fisken said: 'I would say he was not a real person.'

The crypt, on the east side of the chapel, can be a cold and eerie place, and some visitors have refused point blank to enter after paying their entrance fee to the chapel.

An odd happening took place in the crypt during the presentation of *The Masque of Rosslyn* which was performed by the Glen Theatre amateur dramatic group as part of the fringe festivities at the Edinburgh Festival. A cast of 50, many of them local people, recreated Rosslyn's history in the colourful production, which was written, directed and produced by Mrs Fisken.

The performance took place in the chapel while the cast gathered in the crypt below. Mr Fisken, who was responsible for the lighting effects, sat with two of the cast members as the apprentice's murder scene was enacted in the chapel. Suddenly, a freak draught, mounting to a strong gust of wind, blew through the open crypt door. Mr Fisken and two colleagues struggled to keep their seats, but none of the other cast members took notice. Yet when they entered the crypt it had been a clear, calm night.

Rosslyn Chapel has attracted many historical figures, and they, in their turn, patronised the former hostelry, built in the 17th century. Dr Samuel Johnson and his biographer James Boswell took tea at the inn at the conclusion of their Scottish tour in 1773. In the next century the Duke of Wellington was another prominent guest. Of all the literary giants who visited Rosslyn, including William Wordsworth, Lord Byron, Sir Walter Scott and Charles Lamb, the one who left his mark (literally) was Robert Burns. True, Scott wrote hauntingly in *The Lay of the Last Minstrel*

of the knights of Rosslyn interred in full armour in the chapel
vaults. But Burns was so delighted with the hostel's legendary
hostess, Mrs Annie Wilson, that he scratched an epigram on a
pewter plate.

According to Robert Chambers, the Edinburgh diarist and
publisher, the poet and his artist friend, Alexander Nasmyth, had
breakfasted at the inn after a ramble in the Pentlands in order to
clear their heads. The ramble sharpened their appetites.

Here is a version of Burns epigram:

> *My blessings on you, sonsie wife!*
> *I ne'er was here before;*
> *You've gien us walth for horn and knife,*
> *Nae heart could wish for more.*
>
> *Heaven keep you free frae care and strife,*
> *Till far ayont fourscore;*
> *And while I toddle on through life,*
> *I'll ne'er gang by your door!*

Apart from being mine hostess, Annie also acted as official
chapel guide. Her pen portrait appeared in the *Gentlemen's
Magazine* in September 1817. The rough etching shows Annie,
wearing a mutch, shawl and apron, and bearing a rod, which she
used to indicate the architectural wonders of the place, as well as
the protagonists in the apprentice-lad drama.

Annie, who boasted of having 'puttit three gude men anunder
the yearth', was described by the writer as a 'venerable damsel of
Caledonian nativity'. He ungallantly describes her harsh and
discordant accent as being 'quite unintelligible' to an English ear.

During the time Mrs Fisken was chapel curator she and her
family lived in the former inn, but for six months in 1992 they
moved out as repairs were carried out. The original foundations
were exposed so they took up temporary residence in a nearby
cottage.

One night Andrew Fisken was working alone in the former inn when the apparition of an old woman appeared on the stairs. He was stripping banisters of varnish and was seated halfway up the flight of stairs leading to the first landing. He said: 'I started to shiver and the hairs on the back of my neck began to rise, as if someone was walking over my grave.' He turned to see an old woman in period dress walk silently up the stairs and vanish through a closed door. This door led to the Fiskens' living-room, which in bygone times had been the room where gentry was entertained. The woman was wearing a white mob cap, black shawl and a long dark skirt down to the floor. He did not see her face as she had her back to him.

His wife was at home when she heard her husband's car draw up outside. His first words on entering the house were: 'I've just seen Annie Wilson!' Mr Fisken told me: 'I believe it was Annie Wilson, and that she was upset at the changes in her former home.'

Mr Fisken also figured in probably the most frightening ghost story I heard during my visit to Rosslyn. It is a matter of fact that in the 15th century Rosslyn Castle, which stands below the chapel, was accidentally burnt, although during its tempestuous past it was also sacked and torched by marauding English armies, as well as a lawless mob from Edinburgh in 1688. At the height of the blaze in 1447, the chaplain to the Prince of Orkney rescued four great trunks containing his master's writings, and then saved himself by shinning down the bell rope. The story has been embellished by the tale of a knight on horseback who plunged to his doom from the drawbridge after being startled by a horde of rats fleeing the fire. I was told that if you are daring enough you can still see the hoof marks below the outer parapet of the narrow castle causeway. But this is inadvisable if you do not have a head for heights!

The medieval stronghold has lost its former glory but a much later part of the castle is still habitable, and it is still in Sinclair hands.

Mr Fisken was castle custodian for ten years when on a moonlight night in 1987 he was driving up the narrow road leading from the castle to Minstrel's Walk, below the chapel, when he was confronted by an astonishing sight. A knight on horseback!

In the beam of the dipped headlights he saw the horse rear on its hind quarters, as the rider pulled on its reins with both hands. The black horse and knight, who was wearing black armour and visor, were 20 feet from the bonnet of the car. Mr Fisken slammed on his brakes but stalled the engine. By the time he got it restarted the black knight had vanished. 'I thought it might have been a trick of the light so I reversed the car down the brae and then slowly drove back up. But the figure had gone and I was unable to recreate the effect. It was not an illusion.' The Black Knight of Rosslyn has been seen by at least three other persons. That same night a couple saw the ghost in Gunpowder Brae. They believed it was a rider in fancy dress. In another incident a teenage motorist skidded to a halt when the knight galloped across his path near the north perimeter wall of the chapel.

Rosslyn Castle has other legends. A hound, killed with its English master after Wallace had crushed invaders from south of the border in 1302, and the White Lady, haunt the castle. It is said buried treasure will be found if you stand on a certain step within the castle and blow a trumpet. But where is it hidden? Beneath the roots of the castle's 1,000-year-old yew? On the banks of the dark rushing waters of the North Esk or in the glen below? Some folk claim the real treasure is Rosslyn Chapel itself, described in its guidebook as 'a symphony in stone'.

A Knight Templar features in a tale of doomed love at Maryculter on Royal Deeside. In the early 13th century the order owned land in the area and built a manor house, the core of a modern hotel. Today there is a farm, wood and croft called Templeton at nearby Strachan.

According to legend, the Templar was sentenced to death when he broke a cardinal rule. He allowed his Saracen sweetheart to enter the male-dominated establishment. They were sentenced to death, and as they were put to the sword a thundercloud appeared. A lightning bolt struck the Preceptor stone dead. A hollow in the vicinity of Templars' Park is pointed out as 'The Thunder Hole'.

A young married couple counted themselves fortunate when they became tenants of the top-floor flat of a former chapel house, once the home of Roman Catholic priests.

The dwelling, which is on the edge of a former mining community in West Lothian, was comfortably furnished and the rooms decorated with ornamental plaster ceilings. The house was divided into two flats but when the couple moved in the downstairs flat was unoccupied. But their dream home became a nightmare when they realised they were sharing the house with a sinister phantom.

One night, shortly after they moved in, they were in bed when they heard raps and banging noises coming from the empty flat below. The husband padded downstairs in the darkness to check to see if a door was swinging free. He had the key to the downstairs flat, so he unlocked the partition door and walked in. The noises had ceased. Although the place was in darkness everything appeared to be in order, so he turned to leave. He was not alone. Facing him was a great, dark cowled shape; the shape of a human being, but very sinister.

The terrified man fled upstairs to tell his wife. But she was fast asleep and he had great difficulty in rousing her. She told him he must have had a nightmare, and urged him to return to bed. Two nights later they were both disturbed from their slumber. As well as the rapping and banging, which the husband had heard previously, they now both heard the sound of singing and music emanating from downstairs.

The couple, fearing intruders, phoned the police. But when officers arrived and inspected the downstairs property they reported everything was in place.

The next day while the husband was at work his wife thought she heard him moving about in their sitting-room. Three times a loud voice called out her name. She hurried into the room but it was empty. Although she thought the voice resembled her husband's he wasn't around. This episode convinced them they should not stay in their new home a minute longer than was necessary.

Professor Archie Roy of the Scottish Society for Psychical Research, and a psychologist friend, were invited to investigate. It was around ten at night when they arrived by car at the empty house. Their guides were the husband and his brother who travelled ahead in a van.

Professor Roy described his arrival at the house. 'In the darkness with the headlights on our vehicle off, the house, with its windows resembling eyes and surrounded by trees, looked exactly like something out of a Hammer horror film. I wondered what I was getting myself into.'

When tackling an investigation of this type the ghosthunters ask themselves why someone would want to quit their home. It is not unknown for council tenants to concoct an alleged haunting as an excuse to get a move to another house. But, according to Professor Roy, there was no way this young couple, having got their home, would have left without something terrible happening to them.

Further inquiries revealed that the house had a history of hauntings. A married couple who had previously stayed in the upstairs flat had been disturbed by hammering, singing and music coming from the same empty flat downstairs. The wife apparently told her husband to investigate, but he refused. She, brave woman, went down to confront the noisemakers with her pet Alsatian dog.

On unlocking the door of the offending flat, an uneasy calm gripped the place. When she turned to leave the big, dark cowled figure was standing in the room.

Professor Roy said: 'I asked what the dog did on seeing the figure. She told me the animal went mad with fright. It dashed past the figure, fled upstairs and refused to come down. She followed very quickly after it.'

Professor Roy also discovered that the woman's sister had lived in the downstairs flat and would sometimes find that the furniture had been mysteriously rearranged before she came home from work.

The last priest to stay in the house – sold by the church because it was superfluous to requirements – said they were always 'seeing things' there.

Professor Roy described it as a 'classic haunting'.

Who or what was the cowled figure? I suggested that it was the apparition of a priest, monk or nun. Their place of worship was near the former priests' house. 'I think that is a reasonable speculation,' he said.

Moonlight bathed Aberdeen as the student nurse awoke from a deep slumber. Her gaze was drawn to her room's bay window where a tall, motionless figure stood.

The terrified girl realised the stranger was not of this world. 'It was a grey, hooded, monk-like figure but I could not see its face,' Nora told me. Its long-sleeved robes were fastened at the waist with a cord. 'It was the strangest thing. It made my flesh creep.'

Almost 40 years after her ordeal she still remembers her terror. 'I took one look and dived under the bedclothes. It's a wonder I did not suffocate but I did not have the courage to see if it was still there.'

Nora, a nurse, and turned 20, had arrived from Edinburgh to train at the nearby Sick Children's Hospital. She was delighted with her lodgings. She was the only boarder in the west end house occupied by two 'genteel' ladies – the landlady and her daughter. 'When I entered their home it was like stepping back in time. The furniture was of the highest quality They were very kind to me and treated me like a daughter.'

Nora was attracted to an elaborately carved wooden blanket box at the foot of her bed. So, it seemed, was her nocturnal visitor. She woke up to find it seated on the box. 'I never actually saw it move,' she said. 'Whenever it appeared its face was turned away from me.' The phantom materialised at least a dozen times between midnight and 2 a.m., and, after five restless weeks, she told the daughter of the house.

After being moved to another room Nora was told: 'I wouldn't worry about it – it's harmless. It's always been here.'

During the year she lodged there she encountered other paranormal phenomena, including the crunch of unexplained footsteps on the gravel path outside and the riffling by an unseen hand of the pages of a book she was studying.

Efforts were made to get to the bottom of the mystery but the family drew a blank. Although the land where the house stands was developed only in the mid-19th century, the district has a historical connection with King Robert the Bruce, who granted the old Stocket Forest to Aberdeen for services rendered in 1319. The ghost resembled a Grey Friar, whose order built a monastery in the burgh in 1469.

Nora told me: 'The family lived in the same house for 50 years and after the elderly lady died the daughter moved. I understand she was plagued by strange noises, and it seemed as though the ghost was annoyed at the prospect of the daughter moving.'

The ghost of a monk haunted the site of a 13th-century Carmelite friary earmarked for residential flats elsewhere in Aberdeen.

Archaeologists were carrying out a 'dig' at the Green, an early focus of life in the burgh, when odd things began occurring in the neighbouring Old King's Highway Pub and the motor-cycle shop next door.

Yellowing skulls and bones of men, women and children, dating back 600 years, were unearthed, and some bore signs of violence. After this grisly find the publican reported a 'strange presence', but a young storeman next door received a big fright.

Mark Griffiths was in the upper stockroom when he saw the figure of a monk. It appeared solid and was dressed in a brown or grey cloak. The Carmelites, an order of begging friars, were known as the White Friars because of their dress but they later changed to a dark brown habit. Mark told me: 'Although it was hooded I could see its face – it was the face of an old man.' The apparition vanished in seconds. Badly shaken, Mark blurted out his story to his employer, who confirmed the incident. The ghostly monk could be Brother John Tulford, head of the White Friars when the monastery was ransacked during the Reformation. At least he and his brethren survived the outrage. Brother Francis of the nearby Trinitarian monastery was not so lucky. He was butchered and his corpse tossed into the burning ruin.

A hallowed spot in Buchan is the arched ruins of the Cistercian Abbey of Deer, standing in a valley between Saplinbrae and Aikey Brae, where one of the greatest horse fairs in Scotland was held. The small, cruciform church stood virtually untouched until the last century when the madcap Admiral Ferguson pillaged the stones to build a mausoleum on his Pitfour estate.

The A950, Peterhead to New Pitsligo road, runs past the abbey and it was here in 1929 that teenage friends out for an evening stroll saw a spectral monk. Mrs Margaret Robertson and her friend set out from the nearby village of Mintlaw and had reached a low stone parapet of a bridge where a stream crosses the road opposite Saplinbrae House.

As the couple sat talking on that moonless but starry night 'there was swishing noise like a breeze blowing through the trees'. A tall man dressed in a long dark coat or cloak, with either a hood or shawl on his head, walked down the middle of the road. 'His face was just a grey blur,' recalled Mrs Robertson,' but you could see his feet, which looked very large. He walked past without any noise. It was a shadowy figure and we both watched till it disappeared in the dark.'

Margaret turned to her startled companion. 'What on earth was that?' she asked. 'We were very afraid,' she told me.

A motor car appeared moments later but there was no sign of the mysterious monk in its headlights. The road ahead was deserted.

Mrs Robertson said: 'I believe the figure was dressed the way monks in the abbey dressed. I never sat on that bridge again and whenever I went past the spot on my bicycle I pedalled very fast. Since that night I never dismiss stories by people who claim they've seen a ghost.'

Shortly after her creepy encounter she spoke to a cyclist who had to swerve violently at night to avoid colliding 'with a huge black thing' on the same stretch of road. 'By God,' the man told her, 'I didn't half put a spurt on after that!'

Ghost monks and nuns, like most road phantoms, show a blatant disregard for the rules of the road. An Elgin man, Alexander McIntosh, recalled his panic when, as boy of nine, a 'smoky-grey' apparition of a nun floated towards him down the town's Lossie Wynd. Its face was a blur and it had no feet. But it wasn't the ghost that filled him with horror. He was more concerned that a motor car was fast approaching and the driver seemed oblivious of the obstacle in the road. 'It's going to run it down,' thought Alexander. The car passed through the apparition which melted away. The wee boy was on his own at the time but he wasted no time in rushing home to tell his parents. They believed him, and so too have many of his friends when he describes that day in 1931 when a ghost was knocked down by a car.

Almost 50 years later an Elgin woman had a far more chilling meeting with an ecclesiastical ghost. In the summer of 1979 she was walking her dog near the football pitches at Pinefield when a nun dressed in either a black or grey habit approached. The dog owner commented on the cold night air but received no reply. She turned to look at the figure and was horrified to see that the nun was floating inches above the ground!

Spynie Palace, on the outskirts of Elgin, was the home of the bishops of Moray for five centuries. It once stood on the edge of a sea loch offering safe anchorage for fishing and merchant fleets. The small town that nestled below its massive walls served as the port of Elgin, while the shores of the loch supported a thriving salt industry.

In 1224 the cathedral was transferred to Elgin but the palace remained the residence of the bishops until 1686, when the building was abandoned and dismantled after the reformed church gained the upperhand. The loch has long retreated to the sea but the glorious ruin of Spynie Palace rivals St Andrews Castle in Fife as the largest surviving medieval bishops' palace in Scotland.

In their heyday the bishops of Spynie lived like lords. They owned vast tracts of land and they dispensed law and order. Wrongdoers could expect to end up behind nine-feet-thick walls of the dungeon in David's Tower, named after Bishop David Stewart. Scottish kings were guests at Spynie and Mary, Queen of Scots, stayed there in 1562.

In troubled times the palace resembled a fortress. The last Catholic bishop, Patrick Hepburn, strengthened the walls and introduced gun-loops into David's Tower. In 1645, after crushing the Covenanters at Auldearn, near Nairn, the Marquis of Montrose marched to Spynie, where he torched surrounding outhouses before seeking fresh conquests.

History has been unkind to Bishop Hepburn, for he is remembered as a black magician who conspired with witches and demons. It was said that on Hallowe'en a coven of witches could be seen flying through the sky to Spynie. Soon an eerie glow illuminated David's Tower as a sabbat was celebrated in the bishop's apartments, and weird, demonic music floated on the night air.

There is another legend concerning a beautiful witch who tried to gain entry to the palace after the bishop fell ill. Both she and an old crone before her had hoped to administer a cure. The guards kept them at bay. Finally, the beautiful witch, in the shape of a black cat, slipped into the grounds and by the following morning the bishop had made a full recovery!

The palace is known to be associated with two ghosts. One is the ubiquitous phantom piper, but the other is far more interesting: a ghost lion. The beast is said to have been the pet of one of the bishops, and Patrick Hepburn was a likely candidate.

An Elgin correspondent, Morag Thompson, visited the palace on her own in September 1995 when she spotted a huge paw print on the floor of the ruined kitchen range. 'I felt frightened,' said Morag. 'I asked the guide if the place was haunted and he replied that some people said a bishop had kept a pet lion, but he was sceptical.'

About the same time as Morag's visit, another Elgin lady, Karen, was at Spynie with a friend when she claimed 'something horrible' leapt out at her inside David's Tower. Her left arm, she said, went numb for half-an-hour. Karen also asked if the palace had a ghost and the guide repeated the tale of the phantom feline.

A ghostly big cat prowling the great ruins sounds intriguing, but dog owners exercise their pets in the vicinity and badgers have also been reported. Unlike the Tower of London, there is no evidence of a menagerie.

But David's Tower holds another mystery within its gaunt walls. On a cold snowy day the custodian was showing a couple the tower when in the vicinity of the storeroom, where Karen received her fright, they smelt burning leaves. When the custodian checked the basement the smell had gone.

A small, bronze handbell hanging on a wall of Banchory-Ternan East parish church may or may not be the original Celtic 'Ronnecht' which was gifted to St Ternan by the Pope in the fifth century, but it is one of many symbolic links the saint has with the Deeside town.

St Ternan is the town's patron saint who established a monastery before St Columba set foot on Iona. He features on its coat of arms, common seal, and in the East Church's glorious stained-glass window. Until the Reformation his relics were venerated in a church which stood within the present graveyard on the north bank of the Dee.

The monks of St Ternan preserved his head, four volumes of his gold and silver-bound book of gospels, and his 'Ronnecht', which was last heard of in the 15th century. The railway swept away the old Kirktown of Banchory, a settlement which had thrived on church lands, and in 1863 a handbell was found by navvies and presented to the East Church.

It might not come as a surprise to learn that the leafy paths and delightful walks to be found in this historic part of Banchory might be haunted by a monk.

In 1939 a local dentist received a terrible fright as he walked home along a path leading from Banchory Lodge. My informant, Mrs Anne Craig, who lives in Montrose, told me the owners heard a frantic hammering on the back door. They opened it to find the poor man, white as a sheet and trembling. He told them he had passed the ghostly form of a monk on the path. The spectral monk has been reported in the vicinity in recent years.

Can ghosts be photographed? Although the tape recorder has proved more reliable than the camera when ghosthunting (phantom voices and footfalls are a few of the sounds picked up) photography of spontaneous ghosts has proved rewarding and baffling, with probably the two most famous photographs being those of the Brown Lady of Raynham Hall, Norfolk, and the sinister phantom of Queen's House in Greenwich, London.

A picture taken by a teenager sparked off a ghost watch among the tombstones at Alford Parish Church West in the summer of 1981. Sixteen-year-old David Balharry went to the Aberdeenshire kirkyard to photograph the efforts of his father and neighbours to dislodge a swarm of bees. When the photo was developed an 'eerie face' atop of a greenish figure was spotted peering out of a window in the church, which was locked during the bee hunt.

Efforts to recreate the effect failed, and the kirk historian could throw no light on the 'ghost'. But word quickly spread and the kirkyard became a haven for excited youngsters mounting a ghost watch. But the owner of the sinister face wisely kept his head down.

One of Aberdeen's earliest and best known streets was the Guestrow, long swallowed by St Nicholas House, the local authority's administration block. The lost street was known in the old Latin charters as Vicus Lemurum, 'Road of the Spirits' or the 'Street of the Goblins'. It was said it got its unique name because residents could watch restless spirits flit about the tombstones in St Nicholas Churchyard at night.

On a busy summer afternoon in 1982 a church elder was re-laying flagstones, actually old gravestones, yards from Union Street, when he felt a chill down his spine. He stopped work and straightened himself. In front of him was a woman in a long white dress, with a white veil covering a pale face framed by black hair. The figure was gliding two feet above the ground. The apparition moved 25 yards to the corner of the church before vanishing. The elder had a witness. A companion hurried to his side. 'Tell me what you just saw then,' he blurted. The elder described the eerie figure. 'That's what I saw,' replied the other man.

The twin spires of St Machar's Cathedral dominate the skyline above Old Aberdeen. It was here in 1967 a party of schoolboy visitors claimed to have seen a severed hand appear from a gap in the main door. Curiously, there is a tradition that one of Sir William Wallace's limbs was buried in the kirkyard after his grisly execution in London's Smithfield, but contemporary accounts of the dispersal of his dismembered limbs differ.

Finally, the tale of a weird dream, in which a Stirlingshire man found himself in the guise of a monk from Scotland's past. The dreamer was barefoot or in thin sandals, and wore an ankle-length robe. He found himself walking up steps worn with age, and entering a tiny, spartan cell. The only furniture was a table with a burning candle at either end.

In the morning the man found Latin text scribbled on a pink airmail pad which had been left open on a coffee table at his home the previous evening. He realised the writing was identical to his own yet he had never taken Latin at school.

The text was passed to a friend of the family who said the tenses and grammar were wrong in places. But the gist of the message concerned a monk who had apparently been burned at the stake for heresy because of the connivance of a fellow monk.

The message, an example of 'automatic writing', was passed to Latin scholars by the Scottish Society for Psychical Research. The man lives a few miles from Cambuskenneth Abbey, founded in 1147 by David I of Scotland, and now a ruin.

CHAPTER 9

HAUNTED BATTLEMENTS

The bright banner of the Laird of Balgonie and Eddergoll streamed in the wind from the crenellated parapet as I arrived at Balgonie Castle in Fife.

It promised to be an interesting visit for, according to the laird and his family (their motto is 'Truth and Chivalry'), 'Green Jeannie' and a host of other ghosts are said to haunt the five-floored sandstone castle above the waters of the River Leven.

The laird, Raymond Morris, who is a professional heraldic artist and leather craftsman, and his kin, have been working on a long-term programme of restoration since they made Balgonie their home in 1985. The ghosts would certainly approve. The once derelict stronghold is being returned to its days of glory.

Balgonie is classed as one of the finest 14th-century towers in Scotland. It was probably built by Sir Thomas Sibbald of Balgonie, Lord High Treasurer of Scotland. It was added to over the centuries until 1702 when the final wing was built by the third Earl of Leven, founder of the King's Own Scottish Borderers in 1689, and the first governor of the Bank of Scotland.

The first Earl of Leven was the most famous Laird of Balgonie. As Sir Alexander Leslie he was Field Marshal to the Swedish crown during the first 20 years of the Thirty Years War. Leslie was appointed Lord General of the Scottish army during the English Civil War. The great soldier was later imprisoned in the Tower of London and only the intervention of the Queen of Sweden saved him from the block. He died at Balgonie in 1661 at the age of 81 and, following a torchlight procession, was interred at St Drostan's Churchyard in nearby Markinch.

The castle was visited by King James IV in 1496, and by Mary, Queen of Scots, in 1565. The Highland rogue, Rob Roy MacGregor, occupied the castle in January 1716, after his clansmen skirmished with Hanoverian troops and Swiss mercenaries at Markinch.

The castle's most famous spectre is a Green Lady, known as 'Green Jeannie', who has wandered the ruinous 1702 wing for two centuries. Her favourite walk is between two rooms linked by a doorway. She walks in a left to right direction behind two barred windows, stopping to peer into the walled courtyard from the second aperture.

The Laird of Balgonie, his wife, Margaret, Lady of Balgonie, and their son, Stuart, the Younger, of Balgonie, have all seen 'Green Jeannie'. The laird has spotted her on two occasions. His wife gave me this graphic description: 'She is pea green in colour. Her face appears to be hidden by a hood.' She saw the ghost when she let out the family's deerhounds around 2 a.m. The dogs did not react.

Balgonie's chapel, decorated with flowers and lit by candles, is now accepted as one of the most romantic wedding venues in Scotland, and more than 300 weddings have been conducted by 80 clergymen.

The laird said the ghost walked at night but at no set time, yet four years ago one of the brides who held her wedding at Balgonie told an intriguing tale. When she was six years old she was playing hide and seek with chums in the 1702 wing when she looked up and saw a lady in a flowing dress glide down a flight of stone steps before moving to the windows. This seems to have been the only known daytime sighting of 'Green Jeannie'.

The identity of the Green Lady is uncertain, but there may be no such doubt about the spectre that appeared in the Laird's Hall one winter's evening in 1996. The Lady of Balgonie was resting in an armchair when she awoke to find a goatee-bearded apparition –

'grey, like a statue' – in 17th-century costume staring at her! The man wore a wig, big lace collar, jacket with lace cuffs and boots. The figure vanished when she blinked. Could it have been the phantom of the first Earl of Leven? Only a few feet away from the chair is a model of the castle showing how it looked when it was the Field Marshal's headquarters in times of strife.

As well as 'Green Jeannie' the laird saw a grey man in the act of opening a non-existent door in a non-existent row of buildings, either workshops or stables, which once stood inside the south barmkin. His son, Stuart, saw a white figure appear at the window of the first-floor Great Hall while the bizarre apparition of a man's head drifted out of the hall in 1997!

In 1996 a grey man, wearing what appeared to be medieval hose, darted in front of him in the darkened Great Hall. Wedding receptions, banquets and other private functions are held in this room. Brave banners, pennants, tapestries and glittering armour emblazon the walls and minstrels' gallery. Shadowy figures have been reported here and in the courtyard by guests attending banquets.

Other manifestations have included hot and cold spots detected on the walls of the tower by a psychic investigator.

The only physical contact took place in 1996 as a waitress set the tables for a banquet. She was alone in the Great Hall when she was touched on the back. During the day and night muffled conversations have been overheard, although no actual words were recognisable. Female laughter has been heard coming from the hall when empty.

The Laird of Balgonie told me: 'Sometimes when you go into the Great Hall you get the feeling you are interrupting something and you go out again. For all that the tower has a very happy atmosphere. There is nothing malevolent.'

Scotland has a high proportion of 'Green Lady' phantoms compared to elsewhere. It is a curious fact that continues to puzzle psychic investigators such as number one ghosthunter Peter Underwood. Most of the 'Green Lady' hauntings are reported in castles. But the female ghosts of haunted Scotland also come in different hues – grey, white, red, blue, yellow and pink! The colour, it seems, either denotes their apparel or the eerie glow emanating from the phantom.

We all love a good ghost story and murder mystery. Fetteresso Castle, like many Scottish castles, is associated with both, including a Green Lady with a wanderlust. The present building stands on the site of a 15th-century stronghold erected by the Keith Earls Marischal and later burned by the Marquis of Montrose.

The Keiths were true Jacobites and after the Old Pretender, James Francis Edward Stuart, landed at the Buchan seaport of Peterhead in December 1715, he was reunited with his ecstatic supporters at Fetteresso. But when the '15 Uprising collapsed the Keiths lost face, and their property, and by the end of the century the new owner was Admiral Robert Duff, who was responsible for remodelling the building.

After being in the hands of five generations of Duffs the castle was sold at the end of the Second World War and became a country house hotel. Its new owner was Mrs Geraldine Simpson, who told me of the hair-raising experience of her and husband Maurice, as they slept in the oldest part of the castle early one June morning in 1948.

Their temporary bedroom was in a ground-floor turret adjoining a long, gloomy, walled passage nicknamed 'Cellar Street', which ran the entire length of the castle. The bedroom, a former gunroom, was comfortably furnished and although it was around 3 a.m. grey daylight leaked through the windows.

Mrs Simpson was rudely wakened by an eerie noise from the passage outside their bedroom door. 'I realised Maurice was awake, and asked if he heard the sound. He said he did and we later agreed whatever caused it made the hair on our heads bristle.' What they heard was a very loud noise, like a heavy footfall, followed by the scraping of something metallic across a stone surface.

'It was just a thud, and then a very nasty, heavy scrape,' Mrs

Simpson added. 'We were transfixed with fear, and didn't investigate the cause. The sound drew closer and closer but thankfully stopped short of our door.'

Later that day Maurice nailed a crucifix to the door. The couple ruled out hoaxers. While attending a meeting of the Deeside Field Club a few months later they got into conversation with the guest speaker. When he revealed that Fetteresso was the place where the Scottish king, Malcolm I, was slain, both Simpsons replied in unison: 'Oh, yes – he died in his armour and was dragged along the floor.'

Mrs Simpson told me: 'It was an astonishing thing to say for we had not known the circumstances of the king's death, nor had we ever suggested the noise that disturbed us was caused by a body in armour being pulled along the ground.' All this from a level-headed septuagenarian who still does not believe in ghosts!

When Mrs Simpson first set eyes on Fetteresso the owner showed her a skull and a handful of bones which he claimed were Malcolm's remains.

The bones were unearthed by workmen in 1822 from a grassy mound known as Malcolm's Mount, on the edge of Stonehaven, the legendary resting place of the ancient king. What they had actually found was a Bronze Age burial chamber, the site of which is now in a private garden, while the stone coffin and its human remains are in an Aberdeen museum.

Pictish chroniclers, however, wrote that Malcolm was killed at 'Fodresart', present-day Fetteresso, and it might have been his corpse that was being dragged within earshot of the terrified Simpsons.

Maurice Simpson, now deceased, spent an earlier sleepless night as a result of unexplained footsteps. Before they married Mr Simpson slept in a room on the west wing . He was the only person in that part of the castle that night. Mrs Simpson recalled: 'At breakfast next day he was asked if he had slept well and he replied he had not. He complained he had been disturbed by somebody walking up and down the stairs all night. He said the creaking of the stairs kept him awake, but the strange thing was the stairs were made of stone. He also heard the swish of a skirt. This noise always stopped short of his door and moved away again.'

Mr Simpson had spent a sleepless night in the 'Green Lady's Room'. 'We put him in the room because it was a very comfortable room,' said Mrs Simpson. 'We didn't broadcast it was the Green Lady's Room. Maurice didn't know about the supposed ghost. It was an old lady who lived on the estate who told us about the legend.'

Although the Simpsons never saw the apparition, a woman boarder looked up from her work in the Green Lady's Room one evening and saw the hooded figure of a lady, with a baby in its arms, cross the floor. 'Can I help you?' she demanded in a calm voice. But the silent ghost vanished through a wall. An interesting footnote: when the castle was being renovated a sealed door was located at the spot where the ghost disappeared.

Fetteresso Castle, stripped of its roof and a derelict shell for seven years, has been restored and divided into luxury flats, but the legend of the Green Lady has persisted. It was believed she haunted a subterranean passage linking the castles of Fetteresso and Dunnottar and a house in the old town of Stonehaven. In 1935 workmen excavated a network of cellars below the 'Green Lady's House' in High Street. They also uncovered the blocked entrance of a tunnel in an area that was a haven for smugglers in bygone times. A lady in a green flowing gown was seen by residents in the house, and it was said that after each manifestation a horrible green slime appeared on the walls. Since she was evicted from her home the Green Lady has been reported on neighbouring roads. In 1956 the figure of a woman in a dark green cloak or coat was picked out by the lights of a lorry climbing the Slug Road between Stonehaven and Banchory. When the vehicle was within a few yards of the woman she vanished before the startled eyes of the driver and his passenger.

After leaving Fetteresso Geraldine and Maurice Simpson moved a few miles north to another castle – Muchalls, which stands shrouded by mature trees within sight of the North Sea. The castle is reputed to be haunted by at least two colourful ghosts – a Green Lady and Yellow Lady, although there is a theory there might only be one ghost whose dress is fading with the passage of time. This might not be so fanciful as it sounds when you consider the fright Alistair Reid got when he returned to the castle after a night out in Stonehaven in December 1962.

The Simpsons had arranged for their guest to sleep in the Victorian wing, and it was 3 a.m. when he bade goodnight to his hosts and climbed the stairs to his bedroom. To reach his room he had to cross the dining-room, now a drawing-room. The room was in darkness when he opened the door, but moonlight filtered through the windows. He clearly saw the figure of a woman glide across the floor and vanish through the door of a cupboard which years later revealed a secret passage.

Mr Reid said: 'I felt the hairs on the back of my neck stand up. It was a terribly frightening feeling – one I have never experienced before or since.'

Mr Reid, an interior decorator with an eye for detail, noted that the woman was not wearing green; the clothing appeared lighter. 'I actually think it was a ghost I saw. I have never been in any doubt about it.'

The Simpsons had a visitor whose father had been a guest of Lord Robertson, a previous occupier of the castle, in 1906. The visitor told Mr Simpson that his father was delayed for dinner because his train was late at Muchalls station. As the latecomer hurried to the dining-room he saw a woman in a 'yellow frock titivating in front of a mirror' when he passed a bedroom below his.

On reaching the dining-room he made a comment on not being the last down to dinner but was surprised to learn that no guest fitted the description of the mystery woman.

Mrs Simpson, who never saw or heard anything of a paranormal nature during her years at Muchalls, said she was never able to identify the room occupied by the lady in a yellow frock.

Smugglers used to operate at the cave-pitted cliffs at Muchalls. The fishermen of the lost village of Seatown smuggled gin into the country until a great storm in 1794 wrecked their fleet and ruined the community.

A huge tidal cave is supposed to be connected to the castle by a passage, and legend has it that a piper vanished in the cavern, although his bagpipes can still be heard on a stormy night. The castle ghost is said to be the restless spirit of a servant girl who drowned while negotiating the passage to keep a tryst with her smuggler sweetheart on the Gin Shore. The castle entrance to the tunnel is believed to be beneath the stone-flagged floor of the present dining-room and the owner who succeeded Mrs Simpson carried out preliminary excavations.

The fearful 'Green Ladye of Fyvie' has flitted through the corridors and rooms of Fyvie Castle in Aberdeenshire for almost four centuries.

She is believed to be the ghost of Dame Lilias Drummond, the wife of Sir Alexander Seton, a notable laird and godson of Mary, Queen of Scots. Her sudden appearance was said to be a harbinger of death and disaster. Don't mock! A former laird, Alexander (Alick) Gordon, saw the ghost before his elder brother Cosmo died in 1879, and again on his own deathbed a few years later. Dame Lilias is also said to haunt another former Seton property, Pinkie House, at Musselburgh.

Fyvie's charter room is said to be the coldest room in the castle and on my last visit the room lighting inexplicably failed. I was told that some visitors grow uncomfortable when entering the room. Other ghostly horrors at Fyvie through the years have included a cold hand that wakened guests; unexplained footsteps; stifled shrieks in the dark; a secret chamber; the curse of the 'Weeping Stones' (one is exhibited in the charter room) and indelible bloodstains on the floor of the Douglas Room, the former 'Murder Room', a favourite haunt of the Green Lady.

In 1920 a flurry of psychic activity was reported by castle staff. One maid reported a rival to the 'Green Ladye', a woman in a wide, white flowing gown who 'sailed' across her room and vanished into a door. In more recent times a woman visitor told a castle guide she had seen a ghostly lady in the Gordon Bedroom.

'Do you believe in ghosts?' I asked June, Marchioness of Aberdeen and Temair. 'I have to, don't I,' she replied. Lady Aberdeen had a frightening encounter with the eponymous ghost in the Green Lady's Room at 16th-century Crathes Castle, near Banchory, on Royal Deeside. The room is reputed to be haunted by a green-robed woman nursing a baby. There is an echo of the Fetteresso Castle ghost here. Indeed, folklore is full of stories concerning wronged women who return to haunt a castle.

At Crathes tradition has it that a young woman under the protection of the laird became the mother of a child fathered by his servant. Mother and child mysteriously disappeared and the disgraced father left the castle never to be seen again. The Green Lady haunted the room for years and the 16th laird, Sir Alexander Burnett, might not have been frightened of man, beast or Jacobite, but he suffered from a terrible affliction, 'boodie fear', a terror of ghosts.

In the 19th century alterations in the haunted room brought to light a child's skeleton in a small recess below the hearthstone.

Lady Aberdeen stayed overnight at the castle with her husband, the fourth Marquess, soon after the Second World War. She awoke to find a strange shape glide across the room at the foot of her bed. 'It resembled a luminous block of ice,' she recalled. 'I had the impression it carried a candle. The object had no human shape but moved like a human walking. It was accompanied by a smaller apparition.' Lady Aberdeen was gripped by a sudden icy chill as the apparition walked into a wall. Her husband, who is now deceased, was fast asleep and did not see the ghost.

Lady Aberdeen, who came to live in North-east Scotland near the end of the war, knew nothing of the Green Lady legend until the following morning. But it was not her last encounter with the paranormal, as we shall see in the next chapter.

Castle guides have told me that overseas visitors with no

knowledge of the Green Lady have refused point-blank to enter the room. On one occasion a guide 'felt something' brush past her.

During the Second World War the castle was used as a military hospital. James Burnett, the 26th Laird of Leys, and his family no longer live in the castle. It is now in the care of the National Trust for Scotland. He never slept in the haunted room but I can assure you he does not suffer from 'boodie fear'.

Another legend surrounds the ghost's real identity. She is reputed to be the wraith of a murderous lady who flitted from the original Burnett stronghold on the Loch of Leys. But the evil Lady Agnes, who poisoned her son's sweetheart in a fit of jealously, does not fit the poignant figure of the Green Lady. The loch was drained and medieval pots and bones (bones of deer, I hasten to add) were salvaged. The pots are now exhibited in the castle.

Clare Russell walked through the family home, magnificent 16th-century Ballindalloch Castle, Banffshire, when an excited woman visitor told her: 'That's the best £3.75 I've ever had – I've seen two ghosts already!'

The castle, which has four ghosts, is the home of Clare and Oliver Russell, who moved into the castle with their three children in 1979. Mrs Russell is the daughter of the late Sir Ewan and Lady Macpherson-Grant, and Ballindalloch is one of the very few privately owned castles to be lived in continuously by its original family since 1546. The castle, which is open to the public from Easter to the end of September, is a Mecca for tourists, including many ghosthunters.

Lady Macpherson-Grant and her daughter were once asked independently which room they thought was haunted. They both plumped for the Pink Tower, a bedroom. 'It was really extraordinary,' said Mrs Russell. She has never met any of the ghosts, but several members of the public have seen the ghost of the Pink Tower, which is one of the original bedrooms in the castle. She has been described as a beautiful lady, seated in a chair, dressed in a pink crinoline gown and a large straw hat, although she has been seen without headwear. An American psychic went as far as to say this ghost was the family's 'guardian angel'.

The castle has two other female spooks. The Green Lady appears from time to time in the dining-room, the great hall of the original building.

A poignant story surrounds the second female ghost, an unknown daughter of the house who was cruelly jilted. Every evening her wraith is said to cross the old Bridge of Avon to post a letter to her sweetheart. A fanciful tale? When the old bridge was bypassed by the new bridge the builders claimed they saw the apparition several times.

General James Grant, who fought in the American War of Independence and was a former governor of Florida, left instructions that he was to be buried in a favourite spot commanding a view of the River Spey and his lands. Since his death in 1806 he is supposed to review his estate every night on a white charger. Afterwards, his ghost is said to walk the eerie dungeon passage to refresh himself from his wine cellar. Psychics told Mrs Russell that the ghost stalking the dungeon passage had a peculiar gait and 'walked like a duck'. Oddly enough a full length portrait of General Grant shows his peculiar stance, which perhaps bears out their description of his strange walk.

The lights in the Great Hall of Castle Fraser dimmed as television presenter Simon Biagi, guttering candle in hand, told his guests and audience about the castle ghost.

Legend has it that the Green Room in the Round Tower was the scene of a brutal murder. In the distant past a princess was killed in the room and her body dragged downstairs. Bloodstains on the hearth and stairs, now sheathed in wood, persistently reappeared no matter how often they were scrubbed. The guests on Grampian Television's *The Mysterious North* could throw no fresh light on the alleged haunting. What is the truth?

In 1976, when the property was handed over to the National Trust for Scotland, I spoke to the previous owners, Major Michael Smiley, and his wife, Lavinia, about the haunting. Mrs Smiley said that the legend, like all good stories, improved with retelling, and that it was probable that the stone staircase was encased in wood to improve the warmth and comfort of the castle. The identity of the murdered princess is a puzzle. The story might be silly, but the Smileys, who both died in 1991, said the castle had a 'friendly presence', which certainly rules out any bloody deed in the past.

In recent years a researcher working late at night in the library felt the weight of an invisible hand on his shoulder as if its owner was reminding the man he had overstayed his visit.

During the recording of the television programme my eyes fell on the Erard piano which had been pushed into a corner of the Great Hall. The piano is believed to have been a wedding gift from Colonel Charles Mackenzie-Fraser, who lost his leg at the Battle of Burgos during the Peninsula War, to his wife, Jane Hay, the teenage daughter of Sir John Hay of Hayston and Smithfield, who lived at Kings Meadows, Peeblesshire. The couple loved music and Jane could play the organ and piano. The Erard piano figures in a far creepier incident than the legend of indelible blood. Mrs Smiley told me how she was alone in the castle when she distinctly heard the tinkle of the piano coming from the hall. She rushed into the room but it was empty.

Strange voices have been heard in the castle over the years and in 1995 the apparition of a faceless woman in a long black gown was seen in the library and in corridors. There is a theory she is the wraith of Lady Blanche Drummond, daughter of the Earl of Perth, the first wife of Colonel Frederick Mackenzie Fraser, of Inverallochy and Castle Fraser (1831-97). She died in 1874, two years after they married. It is perhaps no coincidence that a picture of Lady Blanche having breakfast hangs in the haunted Green Room!

In June 1968 my newspaper, the *Scottish Daily Express,* sent me to Craigievar Castle to cover the wedding of the Hon. Kirstine Forbes-Sempill and London chartered accountant John Cable. The surprise guests failed to show face, which was just as well. The couple had invited the bride's ancestral ghosts – all ten of them! If you don't believe me, when I last visited the castle the invitation card was still on display in the ornate mantelpiece in the Great Hall.

Craigievar's notorious laird, 'Red' Sir John Forbes, forced a Gordon out of a window of the Blue Room at sword point, so that the intruder plunged to his death. The room is reputed to be haunted. Another ghost is the fiddler who was drowned in a well under the kitchen floor. He only appears to those bearing the name Forbes.

While Valerie Blaxter was visiting Craigievar with her family more than 30 years ago an odd thing happened as they climbed the wooden staircase. She was making slow progress with her six-year-old son and his older sister when she clearly heard 'firm, fairly heavy foosteps' on the stairs behind her.

'We were at the tail-end of a group of people going up and I just stood the children to one side to let the owner of the footsteps pass – which he didn't,' said Mrs Blaxter. 'When I moved the children the footsteps stopped and they certainly didn't retreat back down the stairs. As far as I know no one else heard the footsteps.'

Mrs Blaxter didn't report the incident. 'I took it for granted that it was a ghost,' she added. 'My family was used to such things. When I was three or four in India I saw two children who had been murdered in the Indian Mutiny.'

In 1996 a Galashiels woman told the *People's Friend* about an amusing incident which occurred while visiting Craigievar with her husband. When she became unwell on the third floor the National Trust for Scotland guide allowed them down the secret staircase to the ground floor. On reaching the bottom the door wouldn't budge so her husband knocked on the door. This caused mild consternation, then laughter, when it was finally opened. A party of visitors had just been told about the castle's paranormal history and thought a ghost was behind the knocking!

The melancholy atmosphere of ruined Benholm Castle in the Kincardineshire Mearns has left its mark on curious visitors. Architectural historian Ian Bryce, of Aberdeen, took his future wife, Irene, on a day trip to the former stronghold of the Keith

Earls Marischal in the early '60s. Days later Irene asked him: 'You know that castle we visited, is there something odd about it?' She then related how she was roused from her sleep to be transported back in time to the great hall of Benholm which was lit by candles and by a cheerful fire. A door opened and a man in white breeches, brocade waistcoat and powdered wig greeted her. Irene was emphatic it was not a dream. She described the interior in great detail although she had no knowledge of such things, having recently returned from life in Bulawayo.

Ian conducted many of his friends to Benholm over the years and on one occasion a pal refused point-blank to cross its threshold. 'He was genuinely scared,' Ian told me. Perhaps with good reason. In January 1993, when the castle was earmarked for restoration, a storm destroyed almost the entire keep, but not the Georgian and Victorian additions. The castle, which was occupied by Polish troops during the last war, is privately owned.

In a guidebook of Brodie Castle, the laird, Ninian Brodie of Brodie, wrote of the disappointment of visitors when told it had no resident ghost. 'I say that's because it has always been a happy house – and probably it has.'

Brodie of Brodie, who was born at Brodie and whose ancestors have been there since the 12th century, told me of a strange incident in 1889, when the butler reported 'moaning and rustling of papers' coming from the locked, shuttered and empty business room. The castle was rented at the time and although members of the household heard the noises they could not get into the room because they couldn't find the key. The next day news arrived that Hugh, the 23rd Brodie of Brodie, had died in Switzerland.

But Brodie Castle, which came into the care of the National Trust for Scotland in 1980, might well have a resident ghost. In the summer of 1992 the apparition of a woman flitted across the nursery room. It might be the ghost of Lady Margaret Duff, wife of the 21st laird, who died in a tragic accident at the castle in 1786. Lady Margaret fell asleep while reading by her bedroom fire and a burning peat fell out and set her dress alight. Her husband, James, valiantly entered the blazing room and rescued her at the second attempt but soon 'her soul had fled for ever'.

Baroness Strange and her husband, Captain Humphrey Drummond, have never come face to face with the ghosts of Megginch Castle, their 15th-century home in the Carse of Gowrie, near Perth. But they, and other members of the family, have certainly heard them. For a room in the old part of the castle appears to be haunted by two gossiping ladies.

Baroness Strange demonstrated for my benefit the low, urgent whispering she has heard on numerous occasions, particularly after she's been entertaining guests. 'It is so intriguing,' she told me. 'You cannot distinguish the words. But it sounds as if they are having a tremendous gossip. I would dearly love to eavesdrop.'

The mystery voices seem to emanate from a former nursery, but any attempt to gatecrash the gossiping ghosts ends in dead silence. Baroness Strange has absolutely no idea which previous residents haunt the castle. I can testify to her opinion that Megginch has a 'happy atmosphere'. The gardens only are open to the public. They boast a 16th-century rose garden and ancient yew trees said to have been planted when a monastery stood here.

There's lots to talk about at Megginch. The castle was built by the Hay family in 1460, but was sold to the Drummonds of Lennoch, 200 years later. The new owners had a reputation as botanists, bringing back many rare specimens from their global travels.

The castle survived shot and shell during various sieges. I spent a delightful day at Megginch when the laird and his wife entertained members of the Society of Authors in Scotland. It was an event to set the phantoms gossiping. 'I have no doubt they did,' commented Baroness Strange.

Visitors, young and old, ask the inevitable question when they arrive at Corgarff Castle: 'Is there a ghost?' The reply from the Historic Scotland guide is usually: 'Not that we are aware of.' But something about the barrack room on the third floor has 'spooked' some visitors.

This floor was originally the second floor but in 1571, during the ancient feud between the Forbeses and and Gordons, the castle was devastated by a tragic blaze. Adam Gordon, whose father was the legendary fourth Earl of Huntly, sent his troops, under Captain Ker, to attack the Strathdon castle. Margaret Campbell, wife of Forbes of Towie, and her children and household – 27 persons in all – perished in the flames. The dreadful event has been commemorated in the ballad, *Edom o' Gordon.*

Balvenie Castle at Dufftown, Banffshire, which is also under the guardianship of Historic Scotland, is reputed to be haunted by several ghosts, including a White Lady. In 1994 a visitor saw a ginger-headed groom leading two horses across the courtyard before the figures vanished. My informant claimed the snorting of the horses was heard for a few moments afterwards. A disembodied voice, a flame-haired man and the strains of a flute have also been reported.

The red-stoned ruins of Edzell Castle in Angus are also haunted by a White Lady, believed to be the ghost of Catherine Campbell, the second wife of David Lindsay, the ninth Earl of Crawford. Catherine was the richest widow in Scotland when pronounced dead at Brechin Castle in October 1578, but, according to legend, she had fallen into a coma and was interred alive with her jewellery in the family vault at Edzell cemetery. After a greedy sexton had tried to steal her finery she came to but died of exposure at the castle gates.

While on the trail of the White Lady I spoke to some members of the Historic Scotland staff who claimed they had seen her at various times. A gardener unlocked the door leading to the pleasance one morning when a figure resembling a piece of white lace blocked his path. It gave off a horrible, sickly smell, but, after a few seconds, the figure vanished. 'Exactly what it was, I don't know,' he said. 'I was very frightened – but it was not evil.' At certain times of the year fog drifts across the landscape but the witness firmly denied the 'thing' was a wisp of fog.

In 1986 the White Lady was spotted in and around the castle

grounds. The figure was described to me as about five feet four inches tall and wearing old-fashioned clothes – a white flowing dress with billowing sleeves. Her face was 'a blur'. It also emitted a faint odour, like the smell of scent.

A professional clairvoyant who visited the castle in 1994 claimed that a 'powerful, melancholy spirit' was roaming the castle and garden. The smell, she suggested, was caused by embalming fluid.

Craignethan Castle, Lanarkshire, which stands above a deep gorge overlooking the River Nethan, is believed to be the model for the Tower of Tillietudlem in Sir Walter Scott's novel, *Old Mortality* (1816), a thrilling tale of Viscount Dundee and Covenanting times.

The 16th-century stronghold belonged to the Hamiltons, supporters of Mary, Queen of Scots, who is reputed to have spent the night at Craignethan before the ill-fated Battle of Langside. The castle, which is maintained by Historic Scotland, is allegedly haunted by phantom pipe music, unexplained voices and the headless wraith of the tragic Mary Stuart, executed at Fotheringhay in 1587. Her ghost is also said to haunt Loch Leven Castle and Hermitage Castle, the Border stronghold belonging to her third husband, the Earl of Bothwell.

The apparition of a woman wearing Stuart period dress has been encountered in the courtyard of Craignethan. Two English visitors followed the figure, believing a historical pageant was about to take place. Imagine their shock when it vanished before their eyes.

Several castles and palaces connected with royalty in Scotland through the ages are supposed to be haunted. The country's oldest inhabited castle, Glamis, the childhood home of the Queen Mother and birthplace of Princess Margaret, probably has a more fearsome reputation than it deserves, although several alleged phantoms, including a Grey Lady, are enough to keep any ghosthunter happy.

Edinburgh's Holyroodhouse, the official residence of the monarch in Scotland, and Linlithgow Palace, birthplace of Mary, Queen of Scots, are reputedly haunted. The tapestry gallery at

Falkland Palace, the residence of several Stuart monarchs, is said to be haunted by a White Lady.

Royal children in Edwardian times were terrified by the legend of French Kate, the witch of Abergeldie, who was imprisoned in the castle before being burned on the summit of a nearby hill. The late Duke of Windsor wrote of her ghost in his memoirs.

But nearby Balmoral Castle, the holiday home of the royal family since the days of Queen Victoria and Prince Albert, would appear to be spook-free. A check of royal archives revealed no single haunting at Balmoral, or at Craigowan, another royal residence on the estate. Birkhall House itself, the Queen Mother's holiday retreat, built on the banks of the River Muick in Jacobean times, is not haunted. Her Highland home at Castle of Mey has a Green Lady, the daughter of a Sinclair earl who plunged to her death from a window.

The original name of Birkhall was Sterin, Gaelic for 'stepping stones'. According to a legend, the White Lady of Sterin, the banshee of the Gordon family, haunts the grounds. Her appearance is a harbinger of death and she made her last appearance on the death of Queen Victoria in January 1901, but the claim is untrustworthy. A 1926 account described how the ghost flitted through the grounds of Birkhall before vanishing with a shriek into the misty waters of the River Muick.

In 1868, seven years after Prince Albert's death, his grieving widow, Queen Victoria, carried out her late husband's wish and built a granite lodge at the royal family's favourite picnic spot on the western shore of Loch Muick, a few miles south of Balmoral Castle. The lodge was called Glas-allt-Shiel, (shelter by the grey burn) after the stream that tumbles down the craggy mountainside to the loch below. But to Victoria it was 'The Widow's House'.

She found peace and seclusion in this remote, haunted spot as she struggled to rebuild her shattered life. On her first night in the new house she wrote in her journal that she had a strong feeling that she would see her 'darling husband' there.

While researching his book, *Victoria in the Highlands,* author

David Duff and his wife strolled the pebbly shore in front of the royal residence, which was on Abergeldie land until bought by King George VI in 1950.

When the book was published in 1968 it was claimed by an Aberdeen newspaper that the author's wife had encountered Queen Victoria's ghost during the visit. I contacted Mr Duff in 1996 in the hope he might throw some light on the alleged haunting. 'It is now a long time since the experience,' said Mr Duff, now a widower. 'Nevertheless the impression is still very clear.

'I cannot place the time of year exactly, but it was towards the end of summer. I remember that it was about five o'clock. My wife was in a very upset state when she called to me. She just said: "She is here".'

Mr Duff commented: 'This was an unusual state for her, but she was born in India and I find that this leads to greater susceptibility. Certainly the power of time is greater when it is not disturbed.

'I was looking at the imprints of a woman's shoe by the waterline when called. On rethink, the possibility exists that some woman was on site, did not wish to be seen but was spotted by my wife.'

Mr Duff believed that anyone, alone at the spot, on a summer's afternoon, could well feel that they were trespassing on Queen Victoria and John Brown, her faithful Highland servant.

CHAPTER 10

TO THE MANOR HAUNTED

Haunted Windhouse might have been torn from the pages of a Gothic novel. The ruined manor with castellated wings dominates the crest of a hill amidst wild moorland on the island of Yell in Shetland. Islanders shun the place after dark for it has a gruesome reputation concerning dark deeds, a terrible curse, foul murder, ghosts and a supernatural monster that is part of Shetland folklore.

Historian Robert L. Johnston devoted many years researching the history of Windhouse. But he too was wary of its evil reputation for he confided in a friend that while visiting the house alone he felt frightened and would never return. He kept his promise.

Early man has left his calling card on the landscape. A Neolithic stone cairn, ruined chambers and midden can be found near the house. The Vikings colonised the island. In the first deed dated 1405 the place is referred to as 'Vindasi', an old Norse word meaning 'the windy rocky ridge', and on a raw day with a gale blowing from the Sound of Yell it would be foolish to argue with that description. But the present house is not the first dwelling to bear the name Windhouse. One stood further up the ridge (the foundations are still visible) and stones from the older house were rebuilt into the new mansion in 1707. So, no doubt, as Mr Johnston observed in 1982, the evil of the old Windhouse was transferred lock, stock and barrel to the new.

Who or what was responsible for giving Windhouse its notoriety? The Swanieson family was in possession of the lands for ten generations but their heirs lost the property to a clever, conniving and violent notary public, Ninian Neven, in the early 17th century. Born in 1586, he died in 1662 and is buried in the kirkyard at Mid Yell, along with many of his descendants, some of whom led chequered lives.

Charles Neven (1692–1730) wrongly accused two men from Vollister of stealing his 'quake' (young cow). Instead of sending the men to Scalloway for trial he ordered them hanged on the Hill of Halsigarth within sight of his window.

The most infamous Neven was Robert Alexander Neven (1730–1817), who was nicknamed 'Mad Neven', but I doubt if anyone dared call him that to his face. He was a vicious, bad-tempered rogue who acted like a robber baron. He shattered the Sabbath by firing a shot at his brother-in-law, the Reverend Robert Anderson, who was conducting a service at Mid Yell church at the time. He apparently missed. 'Mad Neven' forced a fiddler, Magnie Robertson, to entertain at a party even though the poor man's wife had died in childbirth the day before.

The mad laird went to the length of murdering miller Tom Robertson at Whalfirth by battering him to death with a piece of timber. Neven went unpunished, but after he threatened Charles Scott at the Haa of Gardie he was arrested and thrown in Lerwick tolbooth, but was released in 1772 with the dire warning that if he did not behave himself he would be shipped to the colonies.

Neven seems to have been kinder to animals than his fellow man. His menagerie included a pack of 24 dogs and an ape. He lavished his attention on his pets and fashioned boots for the dogs. After the ape died Neven outraged parishioners by burying it in consecrated ground in the local kirkyard. They still relish the tale of the ape in Yell to this day. For the dead anthropoid was unceremoniously exhumed and tossed into the sea!

Historian Robert Johnston believed that the deaths of six members of the Neven family in the short space of five years was behind the tradition of Shetland's most haunted house.

The story of the 'trow' of Windhouse is probably the best known of all Shetland folktales, and a popular version was penned in 1863 by the parochial schoolmaster Andrew D. Mathewson. Windhouse, according to the tale, was haunted every Yule E'en (Christmas Eve fell in the month of January) by a 'trow', a supernatural being, in this case a shapeless mass that emerged from the sea to terrorise the inhabitants.

One Yule E'en a storm wrecked a vessel at the Daal of Lumbister. The sole survivor, the ship's captain, bearing a pole axe and dagger, wandered inland and came to Windhouse. The household was in a turmoil as the laird, a Neven, his family and servants packed to leave in a hurry. Food, drink and clothing and cutlery were being made up into assorted bundles. The shipwrecked sailor begged to stay the night. The laird was sympathetic but explained his predicament. No mortal who slept at Windhouse on Yule E'en survived the 'trow'.

Torn between sheer exhaustion, hunger and ignorance of such supernatural creatures, the captain eventually persuaded the laird to change his mind. The captain brandished his razor-sharp axe and told the laird: 'I know of no skull on earth, air or water that this would not penetrate.'

Neven departed, leaving the captain with an ample supply of food, wine, candles and a chest of arms. He also left a bible by request. The guest also had free use of the library to take his mind off the horror that lurked in the raging darkness.

The captain barricaded the doors and windows and settled down to wait events. After the witching hour an unknown force thundered on the walls, doors and roof, and he feared Windhouse would be shaken to ruins. He took swift action. He unbarred the door and chased after the 'trow', which immediately took flight towards the sea. The chase went through fields, across the millstream, around the Lee of Camb, and on towards Mid Yell Voe.

When it appeared as though the 'trow' would escape the fearless pursuer hurled his trusty axe at the shapeless mass. His aim was true for next morning he found the blade buried in a grey mass of matter. His joy matched that of the grateful laird when he returned from lodgings at Reafirth. The captain dug a hole and buried what was left of the 'trow' in the grave.

The legend may be connected with a wooden ship wrecked in Whalfirth Voe in 1731. Timber from the wreck was used to carry out repairs at Windhouse.

The 'trow' of Windhouse raises a smile on Yell. One informant likened the shapeless monster to something out of *The Quatermass Experiment*. But there appears to be more substance to equally sinister stories surrounding the manor on the windy rocky ridge.

In the 18th century Windhouse was occupied by its owners for only a few months in the year, as they chose to live and work in Lerwick. When the laird, Robert Neven Spence, died in 1863, the estate was let to John Walker, factor at Garth. For the next five years Walker evicted tenants off Garth land in favour of sheep, an act which resulted in an old crofter wife cursing him and all his progeny.

To drain the wet moorland, navvies from the Scottish mainland were employed to dig ditches around Windhouse and elsewhere on Yell. On the eve of their departure a party was held at Windhouse, to which a number of locals were invited. They regretted accepting the invitation for the affair ended in drunken violence.

In 1878 the manor passed into the hands of John Harrison who hit on the idea of turning Windhouse into a supply base for herring fleets. He turned his attention to refurbishing the neglected house, and in May 1887 *The Shetland Times* reported that workmen had dug up the skeleton of a large man. The grim find fuelled suspicions of older islanders who had attended the rough and tumble party in the previous decade, when it was suspected a pedlar had gone missing.

Gretta Manson, whose mother worked as a maid during the manor's twilight years, grew up with its ghost stories. Her mother remained at Windhouse for four years before leaving to nurse the wounded during the First World War.

Mrs Manson told me: 'Perhaps these accounts have been coloured and embroidered in the telling over the years, but there must be some truth in the happenings, others having had peculiar sightings and experiences in and around the house.' Her mother, Ruby, said the most frequent ghost was known as 'the lady in silk', because of the rustling sound of her old-fashioned silk dress and petticoats. The ghost walked the landing at the top of a flight of stairs. Witnesses had the impression that the unseen ghost walked three times in a circle before emitting a deep sigh.

The story was handed down that the 'lady in silk' was a housekeeper-cum-mistress whose neck was broken in a fall down the stairs after being discarded by the laird. It was rumoured a woman's skeleton was recovered from under floorboards at the foot of the staircase, but the recovery of the large man's skeleton might have coloured this account.

But Ruby had more alarming encounters with the ghosts of Windhouse. One day she and the laird, William J. Gordon, were looking out of the kitchen window when the phantom of 'a very tall man in a long, black cloak and tall hat' rose out of the ground outside a window and walked straight through the wall.

An astounded Mr Gordon asked the maid: 'Did you see that, Ruby?'

'Yes,' replied the alarmed girl.

'Which way did it go?'

'It went that way,' she replied, pointing to the outside wall. It may well be that the top-hatted ghost had risen from the spot where the skeleton was found in 1887. Was this the wraith of the pedlar whose disappearance went unsolved?

Sitting alone in the kitchen on another occasion, Mrs Manson's mother heard the 'plaintive wail of a child'. She suspected a hoax but the cry was repeated, and then she felt the touch of what she described as 'a small cold hand'.

The girl fled the house and was so shaken she would not return alone that day. During later alterations a baby's skeleton was found in the kitchen.

Ruby and another girl spent a terrifying night under the bedclothes when the manor was assailed by weird lights dancing from room to room and on the roof slates. One presumes they knew the difference between natural phenomena and supernatural shenanigans. Mind you, a lightning strike severely damaged Windhouse in 1898, killing a flock of sheep, so you cannot blame the girls for taking cover.

House guests were never told of the hauntings, although some were aware of a 'presence'. One terrified woman visitor complained that a 'black dog' disturbed her sleep by prowling around her bedroom.

Mrs Manson's father, William Stewart, also had an encounter with a Windhouse ghost. On a journey by foot from Windhouse to his home at Grinds, North-a-voe, a distance of less than a mile, he was followed by unexplained footsteps.

'They uncannily plodded after my father, stopping when he stopped,' said Mrs Manson, who added her father had been 'a very stolid individual', who later grudgingly admitted to the weird experience. 'When he reached home he deliberately went outside again but the footsteps had stopped altogether.'

Mrs Manson did not inherit her mother's psychic gift. When she was a teenager she tentatively explored the sagging ruin. 'Having heard so much about the place I was probably biased. I felt uncomfortable and was glad to get outside again.'

But one person who braved the hidden terrors of Windhouse by spending the night alone in the ruined house is Neil Anderson, sales assistant and amateur historian from Gott, Shetland.

He was a teenager when he espied the mansion from a motor car. As the years passed he amassed a file on the legends and history of this most haunted place. On Boxing Day 1983 he hired an aeroplane and took aerial photographs of the ruined mansion. He could clearly make out the foundations of the previous dwelling house.

Mr Anderson had the overwhelming urge to spend the night alone in the house and about 15 years ago he fulfilled his ambition.

'I told no one what I intended,' he told me. He made his way to the ferry linking the Shetland mainland with Yell and then hitched a lift to the gloomy ruin. He had sandwiches and an apple for sustenance and a blanket to keep warm. He bedded down in an upstairs bedroom in the east wing. The spartan room had bare floorboards and there was no glass in the windows. The plaster on the walls was crumbling.

Did anything abnormal occur?

'Absolutely nothing,' he responded. 'I managed to get some sleep, although the starlings and barking dogs did their best to keep me awake.' It was Mr Anderson who told me about 'Mad' Neven's pack of well-shod dogs. I also reminded him of the 'black dog' that was supposed to haunt an upstairs bedroom but he assured me the barking that disturbed his slumber was not supernatural, and came from neighbouring property across the moor.

The last laird of Windhouse was James Gordon, the nephew of William J. Gordon. He and his family left Windhouse in the 1930s. The late Sir Basil Hamilton Neven Spence, former MP for Orkney and Shetland, who owned Busta House, was a direct descendant of Robert 'Mad' Neven. Windhouse became part of a bird reserve run by the Royal Society for the Protection of Birds.

An equally macabre find as the skeleton unearthed at Windhouse in 1887 was made in Orkney at the end of October 1996 as digger driver Graham Rendall excavated a drainage ditch at the island's finest and most complete 17th-century mansion. 'I saw something that looked like ribs, then a jaw bone, then a human skull,' he told a local journalist, investigating the find at Skaill House in Sandwick.

A team of archaeologists from Glasgow University, helped by local volunteers, exhumed twelve skeletons, dating from medieval times or perhaps earlier.

As the skeletons were removed for analysis, Major Malcolm Macrae, the laird of Breckness, realised his home stood in the vicinity of a graveyard that time forgot. The house, which was built for the Bishop of Orkney in the 17th century, stands midway

between the freshwater Loch of Skaill and the Bay of Skaill on the
west coast of mainland Orkney. Within a short distance of Skaill
House is Skara Brae, a preserved Neolithic village discovered in
1850 after being buried by the sands of time for 4,500 years until
uncovered by a storm.

Skaill is derived from the Nordic word meaning 'hall'. When the
Old Ha' of Skaill was occupied by Bishop George Graham around
1615 the house was a plain, two-storey block with crow-stepped
gables, opening on to a courtyard. The original house has been
considerably improved, and when Henry Willie Scarth, the 11th
laird from 1929 to 1972, was replacing the flagged floor of the hall
with floorboards, the workmen found human bones. All this talk
of skeletons and hidden graves led to renewed speculation about
the ghosts of Skaill House, part of the 6,500-acre Breckness estate.

Major Macrae, who served with the Queen's Own Highlanders,
became owner of Skaill House in 1991. In no time at all the
resident ghost made its presence known to him as he did some
work in holiday self-catering flats in the east wing.

'It was around ten o'clock at night and I was there with my
springer spaniel, Scapa,' Major Macrae told me. 'I was wiring a
lamp in one room when I heard footsteps quite distinctly coming
along the corridor outside. Scapa heard it too, for his hackles went
up and he started barking like mad and ran out of the room. I
followed to see who it was, but when we got into the corridor there
was no one there.'

Major Macrae related his story to his godmother, Elizabeth,
Countess Temple of Stowe, who told him: 'Oh, that's "Ubby".' She
informed him he was a friendly ghost.

'Ubby' is the sobriquet of a man who is supposed to have built
a crannog, an artificial island, in the middle of the Loch of Skaill.
He completed the Herculean task by transporting rocks in a row-
boat and dumping them in the water.

In the summer of 1995 two cleaners had a paranormal
encounter at the flats. They were about to tidy the top-floor flat
vacated by guests when they saw the outline of a figure through the

glass panel in the door of the room. 'It looked like an old woman with a shawl over her head,' said Major Macrae. Believing the room was still occupied they went downstairs to clean another flat.

Asked why they had not cleaned the top flat they mentioned the old woman. It was pointed out that the family who had been in residence had left for the ferry that morning and that the flat was no longer occupied.

In the winter of 1995 a long-term resident's sleep was rudely disturbed by 'something' sitting on the edge of his bed. The sudden weight of an invisible body 'lifted' as if its owner had risen.

After one family had arrived home after holidaying at Skaill House they wrote to Major Macrae about a strange incident involving their pet dog. The dog began howling at 3 a.m., bounded into their bedroom and dived under the bed, refusing to budge.

Frendraught House, set amid a picturesque wooded glen near Huntly, Aberdeenshire, is associated with a tragedy that had a bloody aftermath of torture, execution and a haunting by a repentant ghost.

At the root of the tragedy were the simmering feuds between the Laird of Frendraught, Sir James Crichton, supported by his wife, Lady Elizabeth, and their neighbours.

In 1630 a boundary dispute between Sir James and Gordon of Rothiemay was settled with Frendraught killing his adversary. The High Sheriff, the Marquis of Huntly, fined Sir James 50,000 merks and ordered the 'blood money' paid to the new Laird of Rothiemay, the young John Gordon.

In another dispute the Marquis of Huntly ruled in favour of Sir James, even though he wounded his enemy, Leslie of Pitcaple, with an arrow. Leslie swore vengeance and Sir James took the wise precaution of having an armed escort back to Frendraught Castle. But, incredibly, it consisted of the young Laird of Rothiemay and the Marquis of Huntly's son and heir, John, Viscount Aboyne.

The guests, after 'supping merrily', were lodged in the old tower, reached by a wooden staircase, while Viscount Aboyne was elsewhere. Chronicler John Spalding described what happened that fateful night in October 1630:

> About midnight that dolorous tower took fire in so sudden and furious a manner, and in ane clap, that the noble Viscount, the Laird of Rothiemay, English Will, Colonel Ivat, and their servants were cruelly burned and tormented to death, as the Laird of Frendraught and his lady and the whole household looked on without moving or stirring to deliver them from the fury of the fearful fire.

Viscount Aboyne might have survived the conflagration had he not been stranded by flames while going to save his friends. 'They turned to a window looking out into the close, piteously calling for help repeatedly, but none was or could be rendered them,' added Spalding. All the guests and their servants died and soon the country was gripped by the tragedy.

Suspicion fell on the Crichtons, particularly Lady Crichton, and in April 1631 an inquiry into the tragedy was held at their home. It was decided the blaze could not have been started by accident. Castle servants John Tosh and Margaret Wood were hideously tortured to force a confession, but only the third accused, John Meldrum, was found guilty of fire-raising and was hanged, drawn and quartered at Edinburgh Cross. The master and mistress of Frendraught were vindicated.

It has been suggested that a chalice, the oldest known item of hallmarked silver in Scotland, gifted to Forgue Kirk, was a guilt offering.

The old tower of Frendraught was rebuilt in 1656 and extended. The property passed to Morison of Bognie about 1690, and his descendants still live in the restored mansion.

The present occupiers are A. Gordon Morison, the laird's son, and his family. Although the laird, Alexander Gordon Morison, believes Lady Crichton's guilt-ridden ghost haunts Frendraught House, he has never seen her ghost. 'But that's the whole point,' explained his son. 'The laird never does.'

He went on: 'A number of different incidents have occurred over the last few years which would include guests going to bed only to find their rooms locked from the other side when they wake up in the morning.

'During restoration work workmen arrived at the house to see the doors were shut. But when they parked their cars and walked to the house they found the doors open. This happened a number of times.'

He went on: 'Having moved into the house a few years ago, we ourselves have found that the electrical circuits have a remarkable habit of coming on. Many is the time when we have come down in the morning to find the television or the video on. An electric fan heater, which has not worked for many years, works periodically despite being switched off.' Mr Morison pointed out that many of the incidents could be blamed on electrical problems, but the circuitry has been completely renewed. The house, despite its tragic past, has a friendly atmosphere.

Sightings of Lady Crichton's white-clad ghost go back to Victorian times. But in 1938 the late William Thomas saw her pale face staring at him from a window while he was shooting crows in his youth. A search of the house failed to turn up an intruder.

After the Second World War guests at Frendraught cut short their stay because of strange noises during the night. At first they thought their hosts had been quarrelling but the stone walls are soundproof.

On 28 October 1948, Mrs Yvonne Morison, the present laird's wife, was alone in the basement kitchen, the original part of the house, when she heard heavy footsteps descend the stairs from the top of the building. She listened with mounting apprehension as the footfalls drew closer. But she plucked up courage enough to investigate. The phantom footsteps stopped at the top of the kitchen stairs only when she called on the ghost to show itself.

A staircase played a tragic part in the haunting of another Aberdeenshire country house, Kingcausie, overlooking the River

Dee, west of Aberdeen. Accompanied by James William Irvine-Fortescue, the 15th Laird of Kingcausie (pronounced 'Kincowsie') I climbed the 39 steps and gazed into the stairwell where a terrible accident occurred before Christmas 1836.

Shortly after arriving at the house to celebrate Yuletide, James Turner Christie, who was barely two years old, plunged to his death after he had squirmed free of his nanny's grasp and toppled over the banister. James was the son of Charles Maitland Christie of Durie, in Fife, and the nephew of the 11th Laird of Kingcausie, John Irvine-Boswell and his wife, Margaret. His grave can be found beneath tall pines in the nearby ruined Templar graveyard on the south bank of the Dee.

One night in 1962 his tiny footsteps were heard running along the topmost corridor at Kingcausie. In those days Mr Irvine-Fortescue and his wife, Margaret, left their bedroom door open at night in case their youngest son, Jamie, decided to pop in. 'On this particular night, it was about 3 a.m., we were awakened by the pattering of feet of a child running past our door. I lay in bed while Margaret went to find Jamie. But he and our other two children were safely tucked up in bed fast asleep. We heard the pattering on several occasions when there were no children in the house.'

Along the haunted corridor is 'The Chinese Room', so called because of its Oriental furnishings. Lieutenant-Colonel William Prenville Irvine-Fortescue, an uncle of the present laird, swore the room had 'evil influences'. On two occasions when he slept there his bedclothes were lifted high into the air before dropping to the floor. 'He said he was absolutely terrified,' said Mr Irvine-Fortescue. 'I've never slept there but I don't think there is anything evil about the room.'

The laird's mother, Ruth, lived alone in the great house during the Second World War, and she told her son that every night she took her courage in both hands before going to bed in the haunted room. 'My mother was deeply religious and always placed a copy of the bible on her bedside table to keep away the ghosts.'

June, Marchioness of Aberdeen and Temair, who saw the Green

Lady of Crathes (see previous chapter), told me of the family ghost that haunts Haddo House, the handsome Palladian mansion in east Aberdeenshire. Haddo, which was designed by William Adam in the 18th century, has been her home since 1946.

During the 250 years the Gordons owned Haddo House (it is now in the care of the National Trust for Scotland) several of the family met an untimely end. In 1791 Lord Haddo, the father of the future British Prime Minister, George, the fourth Earl of Aberdeen, was killed in a riding accident at Gight Castle. George, the sixth Earl of Aberdeen, drowned in a tropical storm while working incognito on a sailing-ship bound for Australia. But it is the victim of another tragic accident who haunts Haddo.

In 1909 Archie Gordon, Lord Archibald Gordon, the youngest son of the first Marquess of Aberdeen and Temair, was killed in a motor-car accident. His ghost was seen in the Premier's Bedroom in the 1950s by Lady Aberdeen's late aunt, who described him as a young man with 'red gold hair and wearing a Norfolk jacket'.

'My aunt said he smiled at her then went out of the room.'

In more recent times another guest claimed he saw Archie's ghost, and was able to identify him from his portrait.

Part of the north wing was originally stables and a guest once complained he could not get to sleep because of the noise of horses through the wall of his bedroom.

It wasn't the sound of ghost horses that kept Scottish novelist Alanna Knight and her husband awake when they spent a frightening night at Leith Hall, Aberdeenshire, in the winter of 1968. They were guests at the mansion, the home of the Leith family from 1650 until given to the National Trust for Scotland in 1945.

'We both woke up feeling there was somebody else in the room,' recalled Alanna. 'I had a feeling of being smothered.'

Her husband, Alistair, described the room 'as black as treacle'. 'I had a feeling of discomfort, as if someone was pressing their face close to mine.'

In the early hours Alanna was roused by a woman's laughter, the tinkle of crystal and the rustle of taffeta or stiff silk, as if a party was going on around them, but this time her sleeping husband was undisturbed. Their hostess was American-born writer Elizabeth Byrd, who rented a wing of the mansion.

Elizabeth, who died in the United States in 1989, claimed she awakened to find the apparition of a Highlander, his head heavily bandaged, at the foot of her four-poster bed. She believed it to be the ghost of John Leith of Leith Hall, who was shot dead in a drunken quarrel in Aberdeen at Christmas 1763.

At Elizabeth's last Hogmanay at Leith Hall Alanna Knight's mother was startled by two explosions like pistol shots and heavy footfalls 'like a military man in nailed boots'. The noises were never explained.

One of Scotland's most famous ghost stories concerns Meggernie Castle in Glen Lyon, where two halves of a woman flit through the 16th-century castle and grounds. She is the apparition of the wife of a former Menzies laird who, in a fit of jealousy, murdered her and tried to dispose of the corpse by cutting her in half.

She has a rival of sorts in Aberdeen, where the upper half of a female ghost haunts Devanha House in the Ferryhill district. The Regency mansion was built in 1813 but extended in 1840 probably after a fire. This might explain why only the upper half of the ghost is seen. The level of the floor would have been altered during renovation so the ghost's lower half is hidden. The wraith does not emulate the frivolous Meggernie ghost by disturbing sleeping guests with a fiery kiss!

CHAPTER 11

'CLODDINGS'

Poltergeist! The word incites fear and terror in its victims. It is derived from a German word meaning 'noisy ghost'. Noisy? Most definitely. But a ghost? In bygone days the phenomenon was blamed on demons, witches and unruly spirits. But in modern times more enlightened psychic investigators believe it is caused by the reflection of pent-up energy within the human mind. It is commonly associated with an adolescent girl, but elderly people under extreme stress are sometimes at the centre of disturbances.

Over the centuries Scotland has had its share of poltergeist activity with folk being driven from their homes by stone-throwing, unnatural voices, spontaneous fires or the sudden transportation of household objects by an invisible force. In North-east Scotland these happenings were known as 'cloddings', probably because the chief missile launched at a victim was a clod of peat.

In 1656 the kirk session of Cullen, Banffshire, heard of the mischievous spirit that infested the home of Gilbert Imlach and his wife, Margaret Philp. The couple described how the ghost cast clods and spoke to them. Philp had a reputation of being a witch and was suspected. A few years earlier a case of 'clodding' at Grange was referred to the Presbytery of Strathbogie. The problem was blamed on Patrick Malcolm, a warlock, who wanted a maid to go with him against her will. On rejecting him, 'the clodding and fearful trouble' began, and the poor woman relented.

Seventeenth-century Scotland seems to have been a busy time for 'cloddings' with two of the most infamous cases of that period occurring in the south-west of the country.

The disturbances at the house of Gilbert Campbell, a weaver, in Glenluce, close to Luce Bay, Wigtownshire, were blamed on a curse. A tinker, Alexander Agnew, called at the house but was sent packing. Insulted, he threatened the family with misfortune.

In the beginning, the invisible force worked its woe on Campbell's older offspring, Tom, a student on holiday from Glasgow University, and his sister, Jennet. They were plagued by shrill whistling and a hollow voice, speaking through the girl, which threatened to throw her into the well.

In the months ahead the 'clodding' intensified. Stones were hurled at the house and clothing worn by the family was cut to shreds. Bedclothes were dragged from beds as the occupants slept, and trunks emptied of their contents. The weaver's loom was sabotaged.

Kirk ministers intervened and the disturbances eased after the younger children were lodged with neighbours. Tom Campbell seemed to be the focus of the activity. On his return home with the youngsters the 'clodding' grew fierce, and the cottage was set alight.

In the course of a prayer meeting a clergyman saw the apparition of a bare arm and hand.

The Campbell youngsters claimed they were being thrashed by the spirit. After a final burst of stone-hurling and damage to property the manifestations stopped.

Whether or not Agnew the tinker was responsible for bringing grief to the Campbells during those months of 1655, it was said the disturbances only ended when he was hanged at Dumfries for being a blasphemer and atheist.

The pen of the Reverend Alexander Telfair recorded the bizarre affair at the farm of Ringcroft of Stocking in the parish of Rerrick during a three-month period, and 15 witnesses, including a group of ministers, testified to the violent manifestations.

The disturbances began at the home of Andrew Mackie, a mason, in February 1695. Beasts were cut free and one animal was found suspended by its neck in the byre, with its feet barely touching the ground. But events turned ugly. The family were almost suffocated in their beds when a basket of peats was stacked in the living-room floor and set ablaze. As the poltergeist infestation increased stones showered down inside the house and on its occupants. Kitchen utensils went missing and were found days later in the attic, which had already been searched.

The entity grew more powerful and vindictive and many visitors to Ringcroft, including ministers, were struck by fireballs, rocks and heavy staves. Family prayers brought an angry 'whisht, whisht' from a spectral voice.

Mystery fires erupted all over the farm and the ministers were helpless to rid the Mackies of their unseen tormentor. The haunting reached a blood-chilling climax when the laird, the Mackies and their neighbours gathered for prayers in the barn.

To their horror a sinister black cloud developed in a corner and began to swell. The gathering was caught in a blizzard of mud and chaff and the entity seized frightened individuals in a vice-like grip. The next day a sheep shelter was burned down, and that would appear to have been the last act of the Rerrick poltergeist, one of the most authenticated cases of its kind in Scotland. The belief that an evil spirit was behind so-called poltergeist activity prevailed. In 1825 unknown persons in league with Satan were blamed for creating havoc in a crofter's house near Peterhead in Aberdeenshire. Their target was James Wylie, who tenanted one of the crofts at Braehead of Auchtydonald, outside Longside. Wylie was said to have been held in high esteem by his neighbours, but for six months the poor man's life was made a living hell.

Night after night 'infernal disturbances', as they were described in a contemporary report, drew people from all quarters.

A neighbour left a graphic account of what took place when he accompanied four persons, three men and a woman 'devoid of fear', to the croft. Wylie invited them to be seated at the fireside, but eventually he retired for the night. The anonymous witness wrote:

> Nothing was heard or seen till about the dead hour of midnight, when strange unearthly sounds were heard within and around the house, and as the evil spirit had been in the custom of specially tormenting Wylie in his bed, by denuding him of the blankets, the woman who went with us, stationed herself at the bedside, declaring she would confront the power that would strip the man in his bed while she held the blankets.

Even as she mounted guard at Wylie's bedside, through the house came 'capering' a pail of water and emptied itself on her. The blankets rose in the air of their own accord and fell in a heap on the floor.

Then all hell broke loose. Chairs and tables began to dance everywhere through the house, crockery jumped about in the plate rack. The eye-witness to these incredible events was struck a blow on the cheek with a potato chopper, while two of his male companions were knocked down, one by a heavy blow from a peat clod, the other from a fuggy clog (a wooden bowl) that came from beneath the kitchen table. Every movable object, particularly the peat clods, whirled through the house, causing mounting panic.

'Poor Wylie was roughly handled in his bed and, screaming fearfully, so was the woman, who had lost her courage after she saw the pail of water empty itself upon her.'

The commotion settled, and for about an hour everything was quiet, during which time the investigators searched the house in the hope of finding the culprit.

'During this lull some of our party left,' the witness continued, 'but I and another two remained, when the uproar again continued, and went on as before, and only ceased for the day towards morning.'

Newcomers arrived at Wylie's each evening. Even doctors, and ministers clutching bibles, tried to stop the 'clodding', but they too were exposed to the fury. 'All returned convinced that the devil's agents were at work here.'

It was not until Wylie quit the place and died soon after that there was peace and quietness within the walls of the house, which still exists, and was for many years after the haunting known as 'Boodie Brae', or 'hill of the ghost'.

In 1838 rural communities in North-east Scotland recited a popular poem, *The De'il o' Baldarroch,* at their firesides. It was based on a 'clodding' at the farm of Baldarroch, in the parish of Crathes in Royal Deeside.

A verse from Alexander Walker's poem caught the atmosphere:

> *The spoons an' dishes, knives and forks,*
> *They frisked aboot as light as corks,*
> *An' cups an' ladles joined the dancing,*
> *An' thro' the house they a' gaed prancing.*

The turmoil at Baldarroch, Gaelic for 'settlement in the oaks', was classic poltergeist infestation. Horses were unharnessed by an invisible agent; a hail of stones, peat, potatoes and other missiles were hurled through the farmhouse at all hours of the day and night.

Farmyard implements were not found in the morning where they had been deposited the previous night. Cooking utensils were disarranged and found elsewhere and furniture was moved. But as news of the 'clodding' spread incidents became even more colourful with retelling. Spades, it was claimed, scraped and cleaned the 'greeps' (iron-pronged fork) in the stables, without human help; peats in the stack flitted from place to place and newly washed linen and clothing were removed from the drying green and pitched on to the farmhouse roof. But it was solemnly denied that the milk churn had danced a jig around the farmer 'like a Newfoundland dog'!

The haunting went on for weeks until Sir Thomas Burnett of Crathes Castle, ordered an investigation. When the 'ghosthunters' arrived at the farmhouse they found a group of persons 'with long faces' in the kitchen.

James Thomson, a mason, assured them that the disturbances were authentic. He told them the previous night he had seen a wooden spurtle come through the stone chimney brace and fly through the house. He had kept watch in the attic when a shoe ran along the 'crap o' the wa" – the space between the top of the wall and the unceiled roof – but he was unable to field it. And while taking a pinch of snuff a stone struck the snuffbox, snapping shut the lid, and bruised his fingers.

The investigators took these revelations with a pinch of salt.

They suspected a young servant girl of fabricating the disturbances but they departed the house in a hurry when their accusation visibly annoyed the assembled group.

The parish minister and the laird's brother visited Baldarroch. The suspected servant was in the kitchen scrubbing potatoes in a tub of water, and they later claimed that by sleight of hand she made the tatties squirt across the floor.

A report was sent to the procurator-fiscal in Stonehaven and the servant and another lass, suspected of assisting her in the cantrips, together with witnesses, were summoned to the county town. No record of the proceedings exist but whatever the outcome the 'clodding' seems to have died out.

It was later rumoured there had been a plot by jealous relatives to wrest the tenancy of Baldarroch away from the farmer. It had been hoped the elaborate hoax would prey on the farmer's superstitious fears and force him to leave.

On a visit to the Kincardineshire Mearns in the late 18th century Sir Walter Scott was told by the Reverend Walker, minister at Dunnottar, of a country girl who had mastered the practice of throwing stones, turf, and other missiles, with such dexterity, that it was a long time before it was realised supernatural forces were not at work.

Even if the 'kitchie dames' at Baldarroch had 'helped' the 'clodding' it does not fully elucidate the mystery. It would have been difficult to fabricate the wealth of phenomena without the farmer or some other witness becoming suspicious and catching the perpetrators in the act.

Shetland had a disturbing poltergeist case in the 19th century. It took place in the schoolhouse at Ollaberry, a small community 36 miles north of Lerwick, and the focus of the strange and violent outbursts were the schoolmaster, James Manson, and his large family.

Manson, who taught at the school next door to his home from 1877 to 1888, came from Sullom Voe, while his wife, Andrea Cluness, was from Yell. Seven of their family were born in the schoolhouse.

Although the story of the 'Ollaberry Trowie' has been exaggerated and embellished over the years, it would appear the family was tormented without respite. In the general confusion pots and pans were hurled across the kitchen; crockery was smashed and articles of clothing ripped to pieces. Loud thumps and terrifying shrieks were heard at all hours and bed covers and linen damaged. Things took a sinister turn when persons were thrown across rooms and some of the youngsters sustained cuts and bruises.

A local man who prided himself on his great strength said he would thwart the 'trowie'. He sat clutching a little girl in his lap but he was unable to prevent her from being torn from his grasp.

The Mansons employed a day girl from a neighbouring parish, and she too became a target of the poltergeist, although she stuck by her employers.

It was said the activity centred on the servant but always ceased when she crossed a bridge spanning a burn, which perhaps gave rise to the belief that witchcraft was to blame.

An old woman who lived nearby was suspected of working woe. According to one version the local minister, after failing to rid the house of the poltergeist, suggested the Mansons invite the woman to their home. After accepting the Mansons' hospitality, he said, they should throw a burning peat after her to ward off evil spirits.

It was left to Mrs Manson to perform the bizarre ritual. She did so with reckless gusto for the missile set fire to the erstwhile guest's mutch! There was no more trouble after that.

But after making inquiries in the Ollaberry area I believe the old woman, who did exist, was much maligned and the innocent party in the strange affair. The upheaval was probably attributable to the presence of an adolescent Manson child or perhaps even their unfortunate maid.

In Britain there was a wave of support for spiritualism after the horrors of the First World War. In Aberdeen, as elsewhere, bereaved mothers, wives and daughters, flocked to seances.

So in January 1920, following poltergeist activity in a cottage in Gordon Place, a city centre backwater, a group of spiritualists was instrumental in getting rid of a troublesome entity.

The tenants of the house were laundry vanman, Alexander Urquhart, a former soldier, and his wife and their four children, one of whom, John, a 14-year-old invalid, seemed to be the focus of unwelcome attention.

The first 'visitation' lasted nine hours, with mysterious thumps and crashes; crockery rattling in a cupboard and John's bed being raised off the ground by an unseen force. A police officer who was first on the scene managed to catch the lad as he was half-thrown from his bed by the movement of floor boards. In the course of that night eight policemen scrutinised every floor board and brick of the somewhat dilapidated building. One climbed a ladder to inspect the chimney and roof.

As word of the haunting spread, the streets around the house became choked with onlookers, while newspaper reporters, spiritualists and others tried to squeeze into a cottage that consisted of a kitchen and two cramped bedrooms.

Police were convinced structural defects were the real cause, but trapped sewer gas, shifting sand and static electricity from a telephone pole were also suspected.

The Urquharts were bombarded with mail from all parts of Britain. A Derby company rushed circulars to Aberdeen, advertising 'psychic mascots guaranteed to give immunity from the dangers of the spirit world', priced at 12 shillings (60 pence) a gross.

The Bon Accord Spiritualists' Association held two seances in the house. The first seance, attended by 13 persons, including reporters, was pronounced a failure by the woman medium due to the presence of unbelievers in the milling crowd outside.

A few nights later 12 people gathered at midnight in John's gas-lit bedroom. The boy shared a bed with his brother throughout the seance, while the medium sat on the edge of the bed. His parents were also present, but their daughters were with a neighbour.

After the medium went into a trance she began relaying a message from her spirit guide, an Irishman named 'Paddy'. He told her that a spirit of a man was in the room, pacing the floor in an agitated fashion.

Mr Urquhart recognised his father. The medium, speaking in a thick Irish brogue, explained that when the old man was on his death-bed he had called on his son, 'Alec . . .', but had been too weak to complete the message.

Astonished witnesses heard the medium speak in the late father's tongue. Three times the voice called out, 'Alec!'. Mr Urquhart confirmed these were his father's last words.

After 90 minutes the exhausted medium brought the seance to a close. Suddenly John sat up in bed and threw his arms out in his father's direction. He claimed his grandfather was standing at the foot of the bed laughing. Shouted John: 'Oh, daddy, daddy! I ken what it is noo. It's granda to tell you to take care o' grandma.'

The boy became hysterical and collapsed sobbing on the bed, his father doing his best to comfort him.

After he regained his composure John went on: 'I was greetin' cause I was doon in a black hole, and I was that pleased when I got up and saw the licht and ye a'; I saw granda and he was lauchin'. I got a message bit I canna mind what it is noo. I was that feared in the dark.'

A spiritualist announced to waiting reporters: 'The manifestation proves the theory of Sir Arthur Conan Doyle that the knockings are just the ringing of a psychic telephone bell and that once the message is delivered, the summons of the spirit will cease.'

The Aberdeen spiritualists had reason to be satisfied with their work, for the Urquhart family was no longer plagued by the 'Gordon Place Ghost'. However, a number of psychic experts were unhappy with the evidence and attributed the boy's vision to be the 'excited state of his mind'.

His parents were certainly pleased with events for they became converted spiritualists.

The neighbours gossiped amongst themselves and pointed a suspicious finger at John, whom they believed had hoaxed the experts. He never lived down his notoriety while living in the district. Years later, street urchins would follow the sad figure in long black overcoat and bowler hat and chant: 'There's Johnny Ghostie!'

As 1960 drew to a close one of the most sensational poltergeist cases in modern Scotland took place in the mining village of Sauchie, Clackmannanshire. It grabbed world headlines.

The central figure was a pretty, 11-year-old Irish girl, Virginia Campbell, whose family had moved from County Donegal to Sauchie, where relatives earned a living down the pits.

Strange disturbances in the Campbell family's house in Park Crescent spilled into Virginia's classroom and in 1997 I interviewed her former teacher, Margaret Stewart, now Mrs Margaret Davidson, a minister's wife.

Lanarkshire-born Mrs Davidson taught for 30 years in other parts of Scotland but she will never forget the startling events at Sauchie Primary School, which is now an annexe of Clackmannan College.

Mrs Davidson described Virginia as very tall for her age. 'She was a very attractive little girl with long, blonde hair and the most beautiful violet eyes. She was very shy and withdrawn but she quickly settled down at school and there were no problems with her, and she made friends. She was a very normal wee lassie.'

But about two months after joining school Virginia arrived on a Friday afternoon with her mother, Annie, after being off classes for a few days.

'Virginia was sent into the classroom while her mother tried to explain to me why Virginia had been off school,' said Mrs Davidson.

'Her mother had a strong Irish accent and all I could gather from her were that things like tumblers were flying through the air at their home. So you can imagine my reaction.'

Mrs Davidson, on being told that headmaster Peter Hill had been fully informed, went to see him. He told her: 'Oh, she has a poltergeist!'

'I had no idea what a poltergeist was – it could have been German measles,' said Mrs Davidson 'I didn't have a clue what he was talking about.'

Back in the classroom the children were occupying their free time exchanging library books and other pursuits.

'I noticed Virginia with her hands flat on top of her desk. It was an old-fashioned type of desk with a lid that lifted up and down. Her hands were completely on top of the desk and she was obviously pressing down but the desk was going up. I thought, "that's clever, how is she doing that?" I thought there was some kind of suction involved with her hands.'

Mrs Davidson rose from behind her desk and asked the girl: 'How are you feeling now, Virginia?' She replied in her soft accent: 'I wasn't ill.' And all the time the lid of Virginia's desk rose and fell despite her strenuous efforts to force it tightly shut.

Mrs Davidson went on: 'About ten minutes later the child in front of Virginia got up from her desk to change her library book and all of a sudden I saw this child's desk rising up. It rose steadily off the ground by a few inches and my first reaction was that someone was playing a trick with strings, but there was nothing there. At that point I really became alarmed. I really thought I was seeing things.'

Mrs Davidson explained that traumatic events had occurred in her own household. Her father, an ex-policeman who was landlord of a Tillicoultry pub, was recovering from a heart attack, her mother was ill, and the young teacher had not been sleeping too well.

After the incident in the classroom she went directly to the headmaster and asked pointedly: 'Do I look all right?' 'I doubted my sanity,' said Mrs Davidson. 'I told him what had happened in the classroom. I was so embarrassed about the whole thing.'

She and Mr Hill had a brief discussion about poltergeists. Mr Hill took note of the incident and asked her not to tell anybody about what she had witnessed and that he would make further inquiries. That night he phoned to assure the teacher.

Mrs Davidson chuckled when she recalled a talk she had with the family doctor. After she related her experience he replied: 'Margaret, either the child or you need to see a psychiatrist.'

In the days after the initial incident the pupils began talking about 'ghosties' in the classroom. Said Mrs Davidson: 'It was now becoming the subject of gossip and it was not going to be long before the newspapers got hold of the story. It was decided that Virginia must be protected to allow her as normal a life as possible.'

It was prearranged that Virginia would go to see Mr Hill on a pretence while Mrs Davidson spoke to the class of 40 boys and girls. But even as Virginia left the classroom the door refused to close. It took three children to force the door shut and their teacher laughed off the incident by saying it was 'awfully draughty'.

'I then tried to explain to the children that when someone is ill and the doctor does not know what's wrong with them, it's nothing to worry about, as it takes the doctor a wee while to find out the problem.

'With Virginia, I explained, it's really funny – she doesn't come out on spots; things move when she goes near them. It's not a ghost. Believe me, I said, if a ghost comes into this classroom I'm the first one out of the door and you can all follow me. We made a joke of it.'

Mrs Davidson asked her pupils to be kind to Virginia and support and protect her in the days and weeks ahead. The children accepted her explanation 'quite happily' and there was no panic.

As the story of the Sauchie poltergeist spread the village became a Mecca for journalists. Stories began appearing in newspapers about the strange occurrences in Virginia's home. Furniture was said to move; crockery flew through the air, and when Virginia went to bed the cover rippled like water. There was knocking, banging, scratching and so on. The family turned to their local doctor and minister for help.

It was said that Virginia had suffered a great deal of stress because of the move to Scotland, and the deaths of a close friend and her pet dog before her departure.

In the eight months Virginia attended Mrs Davidson's class the teacher built up a rapport with the pupil. Mrs Davidson never visited the Campbells but Virginia kept her in touch with events in her home. 'She told me about the bedclothes rippling; tumblers flying through the air and how the ottoman at the foot of her bed jumped. What I noticed was that nothing moved towards her, everything moved away from her.'

At the height of the case a pupil called Ann acted as Virginia's decoy. She was Virginia's 'double', which meant the former could slip out of the school gates unnoticed while Ann led pressmen a wild-goose chase through the streets and surrounding countryside.

But the poltergeist continued to plague Virginia at school. 'The next incident was the most spectacular,' recalled Mrs Davidson. It happened as Virginia stood at her teacher's desk – a long, heavy, oak table. 'Virginia had difficulty in catching up with some of her work and she was standing at my desk with her hands behind her back.'

Without warning the wooden pointer lying on the table began to vibrate. Then the table, which took two persons to lift, began to hover a few inches above the floor. 'I had been sitting at the middle of my desk and suddenly I found myself sitting at one corner.' The table had rotated almost 90 degrees.

The teacher placed a hand on top of the table and felt a vibration 'as if I was getting an electric shock'. She had no sense of fear, but was concerned for Virginia.

'The poor wee soul's lovely eyes just filled with tears and she said: "Please miss, I'm not trying this."'

This was the first time the whole class had become aware of something strange happening. They giggled and their teacher remarked: 'Oh, dear, there goes Virginia again.'

'Over the week I did a lot of thinking about it,' said Mrs Davidson. 'I accepted the fact that something was happening I did not understand. I was not imagining it and I was taking a much more pragmatic view of what was happening.'

Another incident that sticks in Mrs Davidson's memory occurred when Virginia came to school with a heavy ceramic bowl of blue hyacinths. The pupils had been given plant bulbs to cultivate at home.

No sooner had Virginia placed the bowl on her teacher's table than it shot across the table, and only the teacher's quick fielding prevented the bowl from landing on the floor.

'By that time we were all quite easy with it and it became almost funny,' said Margaret. Virginia's family had caught the mood and given the poltergeist a name: 'Wee Hughie'.

'The children were quick to adopt "Wee Hughie",' Margaret laughed. 'So if anything happened in the class, such as something being broken, "Wee Hughie" got the blame.'

The case also attracted the attention of psychologists, psychics, scientists and clergymen, and its full share of cranks. One day outside the school a woman rushed up to Mrs Davidson and asked to touch her, explaining: 'You are one of God's chosen and would make an ideal faith healer.' She also received a letter from an African witchdoctor, who claimed Virginia was 'possessed by demons', which could only be exorcised if the teacher danced around a bonfire of powdered animal bones while reading aloud an incantation!

The poltergeist activity tailed off in April 1961. Mrs Davidson found the experience humbling. 'When an inanimate object moves when logic dictates it cannot, then you have got to accept it. It makes you question how arrogant we are as human beings.'

Mrs Davidson has never accepted the idea that a disembodied spirit was responsible for the Sauchie poltergeist. 'I don't want to believe that,' she told me when I interviewed her at home in North-east Scotland. 'I thought there was a much more physical reason.'

Virginia Campbell left the class in June 1961. She joined another class after the school holidays and left Sauchie shortly afterwards. She is believed to be living in England.

One interesting feature of poltergeist phenomena involves 'apports', the apparent movement of matter through matter. In the Baldarroch 'clodding' one witness claimed he saw a wooden spurtle pass through solid stone. There have been many more examples of teleportation of objects by poltergeists.

I was shown colour photographs taken soon after alleged poltergiest activity in a holiday caravan in Aberdeenshire during the summer of 1995. The focus of the disturbance was the larder. The cupboard doors were smashed and groceries tossed around the shelves. Incredibly, a sauce bottle had somehow been thrust upwards through a formica shelf almost four inches thick. The glass bottle, its cap intact, was suspended by its neck several inches above the shelf below. Yet the bottle was unbroken! Did the photograph show an aborted teleportation?

The turmoil happened while the owners shopped in Aberdeen, but robbery and vandalism were ruled out. A large sum of money, the television and video recorder were left untouched in the locked caravan. There had been no fire or explosion. Prayer dispelled the 'power of evil' sensed by two investigators called to the scene.

One theory was that the caravan, which was parked in a lonely spot, stood on land 'contaminated' by Satanists.

The owners were rightly upset by the bizarre events and sold the caravan.

CHAPTER 12

CLOSE ENCOUNTERS

Sixteenth-century Edinburgh knew them as 'the foul folk on the mure'. Victims of the plague who were isolated in primitive huts on the Burgh Muir, until they recovered or died.

On this wild, bleak wasteland, where armed citizens trained, and felons were executed, stood a tiny chapel named after St Roque, patron of the plague-stricken.

In 1568, the sick, with all their belongings, were lodged in wooden huts, where they were visited by relatives after 11 a.m. but anyone arriving earlier ran the risk of being hanged from a nearby gallows. In an earlier outbreak a woman who concealed the infection was drowned in a quarry below Calton Hill. Lesser penalties included branding on the cheek with a red-hot key.

The garments of the infected were boiled in a huge cauldron, under the watchful eye of two appointed citizens, known as Bailies of the Muir. The actual washing was carried out by the official 'clenger' (cleanser). The bailies, together with the cleansers and pall-bearers, wore a special uniform of grey gowns marked with the St Andrew's Cross. Throughout the plague years melancholy processions took place daily as the dead were buried in pits on the edge of the city. The plague huts were afterwards dismantled and burned.

The port of Leith was particularly vulnerable. When a local ship, *William of Leith*, arrived from Danzig with its sick crew it was ordered to drop anchor off the island of Inchcolm. Other east coast ports were warned not to allow the ill-fated ship to land its crew. The victims were put ashore on Inchcolm but few of the 40 seamen survived.

As Scotland became a battleground for Royalist and Covenanter armies in 1645, a bubonic plague devastated Edinburgh and Leith. One half of the entire population of Leith died within eight months, and in the last century masses of human bones were exhumed in fields and gardens in the town.

In Edinburgh grass sprouted in the deserted streets. Parliament fled to Stirling. The tolbooth was emptied of its prisoners. The sick and dying were isolated in huts in the King's Park, below Arthur's Seat. Mass burials were held on the spot.

The occupants of Mary King's Close and their neighbours in the crowded, insanitary houses, which towered ten or more storeys above the capital's High Street, were decimated by the plague. Survivors fled to the country as everyday life crumbled and the cry 'Bring oot yer deid!' echoed through the cobbled streets and dark alleys.

Mary King's Close had several name changes, including Towers Close, Brown's Close, and Alexander King's Close. The latter was thought to be the brother of Adam King, one of the city commissioners. It is believed the close was named after Alexander King's daughter, although one observer recorded: 'Who Mary King was is now unknown, but though the alley is roofless and ruined with weeds, wall-flowers, grass, and even little trees, flourishing luxuriantly among the falling walls, her name may still be painted on the street corner.' This was in 1845 when only a small portion of the close survived.

After the plague abated Mary King's Close and its houses were broken up. In no time the place took on a haunted reputation that lingers to this day. Some of the older generation refer to this area as the 'plague toon'.

It was a minister, George Sinclair, Professor of Moral Philosophy at Glasgow University, who added to its fearful reputation with the publication in Edinburgh in 1685 of *Satan's Invisible World.* It became a lurid chapbook running into several editions. Sinclair lost his job in Glasgow because of his non-compliancy with Episcopacy, but he was later responsible for piping domestic water into Edinburgh.

According to Sinclair, Thomas Coltheart, a respectable law agent, was so successful in business he moved into a better style of house in Mary King's Close with his wife. Their maid was warned by neighbours that the house was haunted and she instantly quit, leaving the Colthearts to face the unknown.

They did not have to wait long. One afternoon on the Sabbath the master felt unwell and lay down to rest, leaving his good wife to read her bible.

To her horror a human head materialised before her eyes. It was of an old man with grey wispy beard and terrible eyes. Mrs Coltheart fainted and only regained consciousness when her neighbours returned from the kirk. The rest of the day passed without incident but at bedtime it was the master's turn to see the phantom head as it floated in mid-air with its hellish eyes reflecting the red glow of the fire.

In an effort to exorcise the fearful phantom he lit a candle and began to pray fervently. But this failed to dispel the apparition, which was joined by the ghost of a child, suspended in the air, and a naked arm that seemed bent on shaking hands with the couple! The ranks of the undead were swollen by the appearance of a spectral dog, which promptly curled up in a chair and fell asleep; a cat, and a menagerie of grotesque and monstrous creatures that would not be out of place in a horror story penned by H.P. Lovecraft. The room swarmed with the phantoms until the fear-ridden Colthearts were forced to kneel on their bed. Suddenly, a deep and agonising groan heralded the departure of the hellish host. Undeterred, the Colthearts remained in the house without further trouble. If the story is to be believed they must have had nerves of steel. On the night Thomas Coltheart died it was said his wraith appeared to a friend in Tranent.

Other residents of the close reported strange happenings and the building was abandoned. It fell into decay and in 1750 a fire completed its dereliction.

Three years later the upper storeys of the houses and neighbouring closes were demolished (the rubble was used as infill for the new esplanade at Edinburgh Castle) and the Royal Exchange built in their place between 1753 and 1761. But city merchants preferred to do their business in the street, at the Cross, and the new exchange became the City Chambers, the ground floor of which is now the roof of Mary King's Close.

But the lower vaulted storey of the old close was retained as a foundation for the Royal Exchange, and it is still there, virtually untouched since the last inhabitant left.

My first view of the most famous close in the High Street was in the company of James Usher Thomson, the Edinburgh historian and writer, who worked in local government for 36 years, and whose former office was somewhere high above our heads.

I looked down Mary King's Close, once open to the sky, and despite overhead lighting, I suddenly remembered Sir Walter Scott's remark as he was shown to his chambers in haunted Glamis Castle. Were we also too far from the living, and somewhat too near the dead? I wondered how on earth official tours managed years ago with only an electric torch to guide invited parties. I made my trip down the close in February 1997 when, due to fire and safety regulations, it was not advertised or open to the public although pre-booked tours were available. A few weeks later Edinburgh City Council announced plans to privatise Mary King's Close and it is now a popular tourist attraction.

The walls of the close soar 50 feet above pavement level. The silence grips your imagination as you cast your mind back to the thriving community which lived here. My gaze wandered to a window, where once was heard the traditional Edinburgh cries of 'Gardyloo!' or 'Mind yer heid!', before an upstairs resident emptied a reaming chamberpot on the head of an unsuspecting pedestrian. Sometimes the passer-by halted the practice with the shout: 'Haud yer hand!' The windows in these old 'lands', as the early skyscrapers were called, were so close neighbours could reach out and shake hands.

The cobbled passages echoed to the tramp of many feet and the cries of hawkers, rag and bone merchants and chapmen.

Mary King's Close and the adjoining Allan's Close figured in one of Scotland's greatest criminal cases. In 1788 the trial of Deacon Brodie, respectable businessman and town councillor by day and burglar by night, heard how members of his gang fled down surviving portions of both alleys after their bungled attempt to rob the General Excise Office of Scotland in the Canongate. They halted long enough to hide a false key and housebreaking implements in a hidey-hole in Warriston's Close.

I had been warned beforehand by a friend that the psychic atmosphere in the close had somewhat 'lightened' in recent years. Even so, the close and its linking vaults and rooms certainly gave me an insight into bygone life in Auld Reekie. And Mr Thomson had a ghost story or two up his sleeve.

Mary King's Close slopes steeply towards Cockburn Street but goes no further than a heavily-barred door leading to a roof. At one time the close ran as far as the Nor' Loch, drained at the end of the 18th century, at a point where Waverley Station stands.

On my underground tour I was shown a bakehouse, a butcher's shop, complete with hooks for hanging meat, a byre or abbatoir with its original cobbled floor and gutter, whisky bond with thief-proof door and pulley for handling casks, and vaulted rooms which served as air-raid shelters during the wartime. Psychic 'cold spots', and the touch of an invisible hand, have been felt.

Mr Thomson said: 'There is a misconception that this underground area was lost and rediscovered. Although long disused it was always known to exist.'

A huge oak door at the top of three steps is said to be the entrance to the former home of the Colthearts, although my guide was not convinced by the claim, or of that particular couple's supernatural ordeal. The door had a peephole and the original fanlight. But the metal street signs I spotted were most definitely modern.

Most of the recent psychic activity has occurred on the east side of Mary King's Close, adjoining Allan's Close, which has been inaccessible since 1932 when its upper storeys were removed. A wall plaque in High Street marks its original site.

The haunted area is made up of three rooms, which may have provided living and shopping facilities for the 17th-century occupants of Allan's Close. A case of living in, rather than above, the shop.

Five stone steps took me into the first apartment, which has a fireplace and is the larger of the three rooms. An entrance wide enough for double doors led to another room with a fireplace at the far end. The chimney breast was holed, for tradition has it that a climbing boy, the sweep's helper, got stuck and had to be hacked free. It was a hazardous occupation for many boys suffocated while sweeping flues.

On the left of this room a door opened onto the smallest apartment, which has a fireplace and inbuilt cupboards. Allan's Close itself probably runs intact behind a door and window, now screened with bricks.

The aforementioned area has a haunted reputation, although until a few years ago no one could explain why it was so. Then Mr Thomson was asked to show a group of middle-aged housewives around the close. Nothing occurred until he led them down the five steps. Suddenly they began whispering.

Mr Thomson discovered they were spiritualists and that they had found their way to the close after receiving a message from a spirit guide at their meeting. It concerned a haunted house in the High Street, and a woman in the congregation directed them to Mary King's Close. A woman casually pointed to a corner of the first room and asked their startled guide: 'You know that is a cold spot?' Mr Thomson told me: 'It was an expression which meant nothing to me but I noted it. I never made any reference to it on future visits until about three months later I came around with a group of Edinburgh students and their lecturer, a lady. I simply said the area was known to be haunted and left it at that. The lecturer told me the corner on the left had a cold spot. I asked her to explain and she said there is a spirit presence in that corner.'

One of the students, a young Japanese lady, came up to the guide and said: 'The ghost is a small girl. She is about ten years old. She is wearing a dirty white dress, boots and she has a dog.'

A shocked Mr Thomson pressed for more details. 'Have you seen something?' he asked, but she fell silent and refused to answer any further questions.

'But in due course,' Mr Thomson went on, 'I received word from the college. When they got back they had a word with the student, and apparently the little girl and the dog she described had followed us around the building and left us here.' He indicated a doorway at the foot of a flight of stairs we had just descended. We were now directly in a passage under the haunted area.

A short time later Mr Thomson conducted a group of ten American servicemen and their wives around the close. Once again they found themselves in the apartment where the small girl and her dog was first seen.

Said Mr Thomson: 'I was standing with my back to the corner when suddenly a woman who was facing it screamed and pointed, saying: "There's a little girl in that corner."' Mr Thomson admitted his scalp prickled, but he was anxious for more information.

'I got the same description as I got from the young Japanese, except the little girl was sitting on a stool playing with a rag-doll and her face was covered with sores.'

Mr Thomson reminded me of the bubonic plague that had wreaked havoc on the population 300 years ago. I stood in the corner but no cold spot materialised.

Mr Thomson summed up the three incidents. 'We must take into account that the groups consisted of housewives, students and their lecturer and American servicemen and their wives. They came separately and it is unlikely they ever met to compare notes. Therefore you must accept they experienced individual sightings, if sightings did take place. I have been down here frequently but I have never seen or heard anything, but the stories are too similar not to give food for thought.'

The haunted area was also the scene of another strange incident involving a group, which included blind persons with their guide dogs. One dog lay near the corner whining, while the other refused to stay in the room.

But the small apartment where the ghost girl first appeared held one surprise during my visit.

In a recess in the east wall there was a bizarre display of soft toys, dolls, sweets, chewing gum, coins, artificial flowers and other items, including a postcard with a view of Amsterdam, a pen and a cigarette lighter!

Mr Thomson explained the reason behind the collection. 'This began about three years ago when a Japanese lady, an author who studied unusual phenomena, came on a visit. She was so convinced there was a little girl in this area that she left a Highland doll and a piece of candy. It was to appease the girl, and visitors have kept adding to it.'

How strange, I thought. It reminded me of a shrine. I left my propitiatory gift, a coin, and departed the ghost child's murky world.

CHAPTER 13

AN OLD HAUNT?

In the dead of a Victorian winter the Perthshire countryside was deep in snow when psychic investigator Ada Goodrich Freer and her friend Constance Moore arrived at Ballechin House, above the River Tay, on the road to Aberfeldy.

'The house looks very gloomy,' wrote Miss Freer in her journal. 'It feels like a vault.' But later, after the larder was restocked and frozen plumbing fixed, she added: 'Nothing less like the conventional haunted house could be conceived.'

The intrepid Miss Freer had hand-picked the servants for the three-month stay at Ballechin, and was 'careful to choose persons of mature age, and not excitable girls', but they were kept in the dark about the ghostly reputation of the great house.

The ghost hunt at Ballechin went ahead due to the generous patronage of John, the third Marquess of Bute, a vice-president of the Society for Psychical Research.

In August 1892, Lord Bute first heard of Ballechin and its alleged ghosts from a Jesuit priest, Father Patrick Hayden, who had spent several sleepless nights there during a visit the previous month. Father Hayden had been invited by the owner, John Steuart, a staunch Catholic, to hold services for a group of nuns on holiday at Ballechin Cottage, to the east of the mansion.

Father Hayden was visiting Lord Bute's home at Falkland House, Fife, when he gave a graphic account of the psychical disturbances at Ballechin. These ranged from loud noises 'like the continuous explosion of petards' (occurring in the void between his bed and the ceiling of his room) to a shriek. He also saw the vision of a wooden crucifix and was scared by the sound of a large animal, either 'a calf or a big dog', hurling itself against the bottom of the door outside his bedroom. He was moved to other rooms in the course of his stay but the fearful noises followed him. No one else in the house seems to have heard them. The priest sprinkled holy water about his rooms and repeated the appropriate prayers.

In August 1893, Father Hayden met a Miss Yates, a former governess to the Ballechin Steuarts, who claimed she had left their employment because she was alarmed that 'so many people complained of the queer noises in the house'.

In August 1896 Ballechin House was let to Joseph Heaven, of Mickleton, Gloucestershire, whose wife and family were so scared by tales of the haunted house and its 'unaccountable noises' that they packed up and left two months earlier than planned.

Mr Heaven was unimpressed by the ghost stories, believing the hot-water system was responsible for the noises, although one of his women guests later wrote somewhat colourfully of hearing 'violent knockings, shrieks and groans', and of sightings of a 'hunchback figure which is said to glide up the stairs, or the shadowy form of a grey lady who paces with noiseless footfall the lonely corridor', before passing through the door of one of the rooms. There was also a man 'with bronzed complexion and bent figure' whom two gentlemen guests saw come through a closed door and pass through the room early one morning.

Harold Sanders, who was the butler during the Heavens' stay, backed up the reports. He described how he had tried to placate the younger members of the family and staff by suggesting the noises were the result of bad plumbing or ivy knocking on the window panes.

But Sanders, a slight young man, was disturbed by strange noises, and, along with some male guests, armed with sticks or pokers, and even a revolver, helped mount nightly watches in different parts of the darkened house, where the only source of light was emitted by a candle or oil lamp. However, the bold butler took to keeping watch alone as he 'did not want to run the risk of being shot for a ghost'.

To deter hoaxers the door of a room was coated with flour and a trip wire stretched across the threshold.

Sanders wrote to *The Times*: 'One gentleman (a colonel) told me he was awakened on several occasions with the feeling that someone was pulling the bedclothes off him; sometimes heavy footsteps were heard, at others like the rustling of a lady's dress; and sometimes groans were heard, but nearly always accompanied with heavy knocking; sometimes the whole house would be aroused.'

During the ghost watches Sanders said before hearing any noise he experienced a peculiar sensation 'like entering an ice-house'.

Sanders then described a terrifying night about the second week in September 1896 after he retired:

> My bedclothes were lifted up and let fall again – first at the foot of my bed, but gradually coming towards my head. I held the clothes around my neck with my hands, but they were gently lifted in spite of my efforts to hold them. I then reached around me with my hand, but could feel nothing. This was immediately followed by my being fanned as though some bird was flying around my head, and I could distinctly hear and feel something breathing on me. I then tried to reach some matches that were on a chair by my bedside, but my hand was held back as if by some invisible power. Then the thing seemed to retire to the foot of my bed. Then I suddenly found the foot of my bed lifted up and carried around towards the window for about three or four feet, then replaced to its former position. All this did not take, I should think, more than two or three minutes, although at the time it seemed hours to me. Just then the clock struck four, and, being tired out with my long night's watching, I fell asleep.

Cynical readers might believe that poor Sanders was either lying or the victim of a practical joke at the hands of the 'gentlemen' ghosthunters. However, Colonel G.L. Le Mesurier Taylor, of the Society for Psychical Research, who later interviewed him, found him 'quite honest and serious over the Ballechin affair', and believed the account to be 'absolutely true'.

In the quaint riverbank kirkyard at Logierait village, no great distance from Ballechin House, a rough-stoned enclosure stands yards from the white-walled church. It is pointed out as the burial place of the Stewarts of Ballechin, lineal descendants of Robert the Second of Scotland, and the Bailies of Atholl. The ancient Perthshire family fought on Bonnie Dundee's side at Killiecrankie. Some members later adopted the name 'Steuart'.

It is believed to contain the graves of three persons connected with Ballechin. Major Robert Steuart, born 1806, who became the 12th laird of Ballechin while serving with the East India Company, died in April 1876. The other graves are those of his old Indian manservant and his housekeeper, Miss Sarah Nicholson, a farmer's daughter, who died three years before her employer at the age of 27.

The graves are unmarked and the space within the enclosure is occupied by three mortsafes, one child's size, which were used to deter bodysnatchers.

The bachelor major was described as an eccentric recluse who was fond of Sarah, but this might have been vindictive gossip. He kept a large number of dogs and swore he would haunt Ballechin after his death in the guise of his favourite pet, a black spaniel. It was said that after he died this was the reason why his 14 dogs were destroyed.

Father Hayden, who alerted Lord Bute to the haunted manor, spoke to a witness who claimed the major's successor, John Steuart, his nephew, had seen a procession of monks and nuns from a window. The mystery surrounding the house deepened after John, the 13th laird, was knocked down and killed by a London cab on 20 December 1895. He is buried in the small family graveyard at the Catholic chapel which stands above the tumbling waters of

Tulliepowrie Burn. His eccentric uncle was not a Catholic.

According to Miss Freer it was said that on the morning of his departure to London the laird was talking to his agent in his office when their conversation was interrupted by violent raps. In his journal Lord Bute, recording the tragedy, suggested that 'spirits came and rapped to him in his room – doubtless to warn him – so that his death was really owing to the cruel superstition which had prevented him allowing them to be communicated with'.

At the time Ada Goodrich Freer, who claimed paranormal powers, and her fellow ghosthunters arrived at Ballechin – Gaelic for 'Hector's Place' – the fine, ivy-clad house stood three storeys tall with attic. The highlight of the pavilion-roofed dwelling was the projecting south bow facing the manicured lawn.

The house was originally built in 1806, but further improvements were carried out, including an east wing, built in 1883, it was said, so that the children of the family could live and play outwith the haunted areas. Lord Bute described Ballechin as 'a luxurious country house, ample, though not too large, in a beautiful neighbourhood . . .'

Miss Freer and Constance Moore, daughter of Canon Daniel Moore, Prebendary of St Paul's, London, and Chaplain to Queen Victoria, arrived at Ballechin on Wednesday, 3 February 1897. Miss Freer, better known as 'Miss X' to readers of psychical literature, was appointed by the Society for Psychical Research to carry out an investigation into the alleged haunting.

The ground rules for the ghost hunt were outlined in her article in the popular magazine, *The Nineteenth Century*, in August 1897: 'The natural thing to do was to settle down to a country house life, make it as pleasant as possible, and await events.'

The ghosthunters were short in practical aids. Miss Freer brought her camera and a guest kept a flashlight under a pillow – 'very convenient for ghost hunting', noted Miss Freer, 'no delay and no possibility of blowing it out'. Miss Freer brought her Pomerian, 'Spooks', while Miss Moore cared for 'Scamp'.

More than 30 guests, almost all with an interest in the

paranormal, were invited to Ballechin over the next three months. The lease was negotiated in the name of the aforementioned Colonel Le Mesurier Taylor, but he was unable to travel to Scotland immediately because of a family bereavement. Lord Bute agreed to foot the bill for the entire investigation.

On the first morning after their arrival Miss Freer and Miss Moore reported hearing 'a loud clanging sound', resembling metal struck by wood, throughout the house and this noise was repeated at frequent intervals for two hours. A maidservant, hired locally, walked out within hours although the factor described her talk of ghosts as 'all havers' (drivel).

In the course of the ghost hunt the apparent psychic phenomena intensified. The sound of disembodied voices was heard: phantom footsteps, thunderous knocking, and explosive sounds resembling the 'one o'clock gun in Edinburgh' or the 'distant boom of a naval gun at Portsmouth' were reported by some guests. A maid was startled by the apparition of a woman with no legs!

Afternoons were passed experimenting with an ouija board and automatic writing. A communicator called 'Ishbel' asked the investigators to go at dusk to a nearby glen, previously identified as 'Scamp's Copse', because of the dog's peculiar behaviour there on a recent ramble.

Miss Freer, accompanied by two men, followed the instructions but only she reported seeing the slight, black figure of a nun moving up the snow-carpeted glen close by a frozen stream. She saw the nun on other occasions, sometimes weeping, sometimes talking 'upon rather a high note, with a quality of youth in her voice'.

Miss Freer subsequently reported seeing the nun in the company of an older woman in grey (perhaps the Grey Lady of local folklore), whom she named 'Marget', a name referred to by the ouija board communicator.

It was remembered that one of Major Steuart's six sisters, Isabella, had entered a nunnery and died in 1880.

On 19 February Miss Freer travelled by horse trap to Aberfeldy railway station to meet the Reverend Charles Shaw of the Society for Psychical Research. Unfortunately she met with an accident when the horse was frightened by the train. It curtailed her outdoor activities and only Shaw went to the haunted glen where he reported seeing a white light under a big tree. The vicar would later see a brief vision of a wooden crucifix on his bedroom wall.

However, a study of the journal Miss Freer kept of the alleged haunting shows it was she who first heard the strange noises at Ballechin; who first saw the ghost, and who always seemed to be at hand when reporting psychic phenomena in a most baffling case.

Psychic activity was heard in most bedrooms, including two on the third floor on the south side of the house. Major Steuart's young housekeeper was said to have died in one of these rooms and it was there that shuffling noises, a phantom dog, thumps, and so on, were heard. The servants' quarters in the attic and the butler's room on the first floor were also said to be haunted.

In the course of their stay guests tried to recreate the various noises, and even went to the length of carrying out experiments on the roof of the house, but the results were disappointing.

Colonel Taylor eventually visited Ballechin, spending five weeks there 'very pleasantly', as he wrote to Lord Bute. While Colonel Taylor felt sure there was a 'ghostly influence pervading the house', he expressed disappointment in the way it manifested itself, although he thought the vision of the crucifix important.

Miss Freer had planned to spend Easter elsewhere but stayed over till 8 April, the anniversary of Major Steuart's death. She was not disappointed. A watch was kept on the downstairs smoking-room, on the ground floor, known as 'the major's room'. It was while sitting at a desk that a black dog, resembling a spaniel, trotted towards her own dog, 'Spooks', then vanished.

After dinner Miss Freer and two other witnesses heard heavy disembodied footsteps walk round the room. In the course of the evening the angry voices of a man and a woman were heard arguing outside the room, but a check revealed an empty dark passage.

Miss Freer did not return to Ballechin until the end of April, on the very day her rich patron, Lord Bute, and his wife, departed after spending two days in the east wing. They did not meet.

In his journal Lord Bute described the house as 'remarkably bright and cheerful, and indeed luxurious'. He said prayers throughout the house and felt a strong presence. But he also observed: 'It was hostile or evil, as though we were kept at arm's length; a disagreeable sensation continued until I threw holy water on my bed before getting into it, when it suddenly disappeared.'

However he heard and saw nothing and slept well. During the short stay he visited the haunted glen and the major's grave in Logierait.

At the beginning of May three Catholic clergymen, including Archbishop Angus MacDonald, said mass on the ground floor of Ballechin House. The archbishop blessed the house from top to bottom and sprinkled the rooms with holy water. During the service there was a deafening thump and Miss Freer claimed she saw the apparitions of 'Ishbel' and 'Marget' on the lawn outside the French windows.

Before Colonel Taylor's tenancy ended Miss Freer welcomed a small group to Ballechin. It comprised Sir James Crichton-Brown, his nephew and another gentleman, who, unknown to her, was J. Callendar Ross, a staff writer on *The Times.*

When his article, *On the Trail of a Ghost,* appeared in the newspaper on Tuesday, 8 June 1897, it caused a first-class scandal and proved a major embarrassment to Lord Bute and the Society of Psychical Research, whose honorary secretary, Frederic W.H. Myers, a supporter of Miss Freer, quickly distanced himself and his organisation from her and the Ballechin ghost hunt.

A war of words erupted in the correspondence columns of *The Times.* It became clear that the owners of Ballechin had been deceived. They believed their home had been rented to Colonel Taylor for sporting purposes.

Captain Steuart, writing from Paris, said he had no idea he was letting his home to Lord Bute and the Society for Psychical

Research, 'and would never have done so had I known. I let Ballechin for three months to a Colonel Taylor, with fishing etc., and it was only at the end of his tenancy I discovered for what purposes and by whom Ballechin had been really rented.' He revealed that Lord Bute had previously tried to get his father's permission for one or two members of the SPR to reside at Ballechin. The stories of the haunting, he added, were without foundation.

During the coming weeks letter writers poured scorn on the alleged haunting, attributing the noises to earth tremors, faulty architecture and a vivid imagination. Grave doubts were cast on the judgement of Miss Freer and her fellow ghosthunters.

Mr Heaven, who was tenant before Colonel Taylor, threatened *The Times* with legal action because it dared to suggest that the younger members of his family had been responsible for practical jokes which gave rise to the ghost hunt. One prank, it was reported, was to drop a heavy weight on the hall floor from the topmost banister then draw it back on a string!

The Alleged Haunting of B— House, co-edited by Miss Freer and Lord Bute, was published in 1899, with a second revised edition coming out the next year. The identity of Ballechin and those involved was not disclosed (in the first edition the name of the house was inadvertently revealed on page 82), but the public would not be fooled.

At the beginning of the century Miss Freer married Dr Hans Spoer, a chaplain, and together they worked in the Holy Land before settling in New York, where she died in 1931, aged 73.

In 1968 Ada Goodrich Freer's role in collecting and publishing evidence of second-sight and ghost stories in the Outer Hebrides was questioned by the authors of *Strange Things*, published in 1968.

John Lorne Campbell and Trevor H. Hall found that the material, which was published under her own name in 1902, was in fact the work of a priest, Father Allan McDonald, a collector of Gaelic folklore, who was a guest at Ballechin.

Hall, a member of the Magic Circle for 40 years, wrote several books on critical psychical research, including a debunking of ghost-hunter Harry Price's investigation of Borley Rectory.

However, the assessment of Miss Freer's character and the investigation of the alleged haunting of Ballechin House does not elucidate the mystery of the Perthshire mansion, which was ironically described in J. Callendar Ross's controversial article in *The Times* as 'the most haunted house in Scotland'.

Did the society spook-hunting party obscure the ghostly truth?

Exactly 100 years after the advance guard of Victorian ghost-hunters arrived at Ballechin, I drove up the oak and birch-lined avenue which Miss Freer claimed was shunned by the whole neighbourhood after dark. I bridged the haunted stream and parked at what remains of the old mansion. The main part of the building is ruinous. It was demolished in 1963 because of dry rot. The attractive lawn, where croquet was once played, smart tennis courts, bowling green, greenhouses and fruitful garden, have gone.

What has been saved is the east wing, built in the last century to house the kitchen on the ground floor and children's nursery and bedrooms on the floor above.

There I met Alasdair Steven, journalist and antiquarian bookseller, who lived in the east wing with his beloved books for 26 years, but has since moved to a new home in Blackford. A wry smile was his response when I mentioned Ballechin's ghostly past.

'I tend to be highly sceptical,' he said. 'But I do feel the ghost-hunters made a hash of the whole thing. They were very ineffectual. Ada Goodrich Freer was behind the strength of the ghost story and I feel she didn't want to dismiss it for fear of losing face.'

Mr Steven never heard or saw anything bordering on the paranormal during his tenancy of the east wing, now called Old Ballechin. When his wife expressed doubts about sleeping in a haunted house he was quick to point out that Lord and Lady Bute had stayed there in 1897, and had no grounds for complaint!

But from my inquiries I discovered strange things were seen and heard by staff before the demolition men descended on Ballechin. In the autumn of 1936 Mrs Mary MacDonald was waitress in charge of the dining-room. She did not know anything of ghosts or such things the day she took her employer's rust-coloured spaniel, Wee Lassie, for a walk.

Near the east wing she stopped to chat to the chauffeur and gardener as they tinkered with a generator. Her curiosity was drawn to a rough flight of stone steps leading underground. The men told her it was said to be the entrance to a passage which had been a bolthole in bygone days.

Mrs MacDonald and another girl gamely entered the dark passage but her companion turned back. Mrs MacDonald inched her way along the stone passage until her progress was reduced to a crouch. 'Suddenly I heard a dog whining in the dark ahead of me,' recalled Mrs MacDonald. 'I got a terrible fright because I thought the spaniel had somehow become trapped. My first thoughts were that I had lost the dog and I would lose my job.'

She scrambled out of the passage to find the dog where she had left it. She is convinced there was no way the dog could have slipped unnoticed into and out of the passage without her knowledge and there was no other dog around.

During the two years she worked at Ballechin – 'a beautiful, square white house' – was how she described it, she saw nothing strange. But she did hear the ladies' maid request a change of room because she was being frightened by strange noises.

On my ghost quest I spoke to another ex-member of staff. She was reluctant to discuss her experiences but claimed a maid was frightened by a ghost dog while fetching milk from the dairy.

Ballechin Cottage, the former nunnery, is the home of Miss Elizabeth Honeyman, the present owner of Old Ballechin. The estate was bought by her late father, R. Wemyss Honeyman, businessman and landowner, in 1932.

One night she awoke in the cottage to find a ghost nun standing at the foot of her bed. The entity was draped in a grey cloak and hood, but Miss Honeyman could not distinguish any features. 'I quite honestly felt the quilt move,' she said. 'I got such a terrible fright.'

A psychic friend who visited the cottage was put in the room next to Miss Honeyman's. She was not told of her hostess's paranormal experience, and no mention was made of the cottage having been a nunnery.

Asked at breakfast if she had slept well Miss Honeyman's friend replied: 'Yes, apart from a party of nuns playing cards in your room.'

'I am not psychic but I have always felt a friendly presence in my home,' said Miss Honeyman.

Of the former mansion's ghostly reputation she replied: 'The Grey Lady is supposed to haunt the drive leading from the west lodge and there have been people who claim to have heard phantom dogs.'

Winter sunshine provided little warmth on my visit. Blades of grass, touched by frost, resembled stubble of an old tramp's chin. In summer the wild garden is ablaze with azaleas and rhododendrons, and the view across the valley of the Tay is breathtaking.

A grey slab of stone marks the main entrance to the former house. In the old kitchen in the east wing basement I saw the original heating boiler that kept the great house supplied with hot water which was blamed for causing the violent knockings as it cooled in the pipes.

On the south side of the ruined mansion I examined the shell of the bow window at ground level. In Victorian times this was the 'major's room', where Miss Freer claimed she saw his ghost dog. Now this room, along with the rest of the ground floor, is choked with tons of rubble. The truth behind *The Alleged Haunting of B— House* lies buried within.

The smoke from Alasdair Steven's chimney hung like a question mark in the chill air as I left Ballechin.

BIBLIOGRAPHY

Adams, Norman *Haunted Neuk* (Tolbooth Books, Banchory, 1994), *Haunted Valley* (Tolbooth Books, Banchory, 1994)

Campbell, John L. and Hall, Trevor H. *Strange Things* (Routledge and Kegan Paul, London, 1968)

Coventry, Martin *The Castles of Scotland* (Goblinshead, Edinburgh, 1995)

Duff, David *Victoria in the Highlands* (Frederick Muller, London, 1968)

Goodrich-Freer, A. (Miss X), and John, Marquess of Bute. *The Alleged Haunting of B— House, including a journal kept during the tenancy of Colonel Lemesurier Taylor* (George Redway, London, 1899)

Gregor, Walter *Notes on the Folklore of the North-east of Scotland* (London, 1881)

Henderson, Margaret *The Giffords of Busta House* (Shetland, n.d.)

Macdonald, R. Robertson *Selected Highland Folktales* (Oliver and Boyd, Edinburgh, 1966)

MacGregor, Alasdair Alpin, *The Turbulent Years* (Methuen, London, 1945), *Phantom Footsteps* (Robert Hale, London, 1959)

McPherson, Rev J.M. *Primitive Beliefs in the North-east of Scotland* (Longmans, London, 1929)

Marren, Peter *Grampian Battlefields* (AUP, Aberdeen)

Ritchie, Anna *Exploring Scotland's History: Orkney and Shetland* (HMSO, 1985)

Smith, Alexander *A New History of Aberdeenshire* (Aberdeen, 1875)

Smith, David *Action Stations 7* (Patrick Stephens, Wellingborough, 1989)

Underwood, Peter *Gazetteer of Scottish Ghosts* (Fontana, London, 1974), *Guide to Ghosts and Haunted Places* (Piatkus, London, 1996)

Wallace-Murphy, Tim *An Illustrated Guide to Rosslyn Chapel* (Friends of Rosslyn, Roslin, 1993)

Watt, Archibald *Highways and Byways Round Stonehaven* (Waverley Press, Aberdeen, n.d.)

Other sources: *Byre Theatre, St Andrews – The First Twenty-Five Years (1933–1958)* (The University Press, 1959); *The PSI Report, Newsletter of the Scottish Society for Psychical Research; Alloa and Hillfoots Advertiser; Alloa Journal; Courier and Advertiser; East Fife Mail; Evening Express (* Aberdeen); *Evening News* (Edinburgh); *Fife Free Press; Forres Gazette; Gentlemen's Magazine; Haunted Scotland Newsletter; The Orcadian; People's Friend; Press and Journal; The Scots Magazine; The Scotsman; Scottish Arts Monthly; Scottish Notes and Queries (1926); Shetland Life; Shetland Times; Stornoway Gazette; The Story of Discovery* (Dundee Industrial Heritage, 1996), *The Times* and various booklets and guidebooks published by the National Trust for Scotland.

INDEX